THE ALASKA SIDE

A Picture is Worth 1000 Words

COLORING BOOK

56 Humorous illustrations of life in
the Last Frontier For all Ages

Gregory Podsiki

ARCHWAY
PUBLISHING

Archway Publishing books may be ordered through booksellers or by contacting:

Archway Publishing
1663 Liberty Drive
Bloomington, IN 47403
www.archwaypublishing.com
844-669-3957

Because of the dynamic nature of the Internet, any web addresses or links contained in this book may have changed since publication and may no longer be valid. The views expressed in this work are solely those of the author and do not necessarily reflect the views of the publisher, and the publisher hereby disclaims any responsibility for them.

Any people depicted in stock imagery provided by Getty Images are models, and such images are being used for illustrative purposes only.
Certain stock imagery © Getty Images.

Interior Graphics/Art Credit: Gregory Podsiki

ISBN: 978-1-6657-6959-4 (sc)
ISBN: 978-1-6657-6960-0 (e)

Print information available on the last page.

Archway Publishing rev. date: 12/17/2024

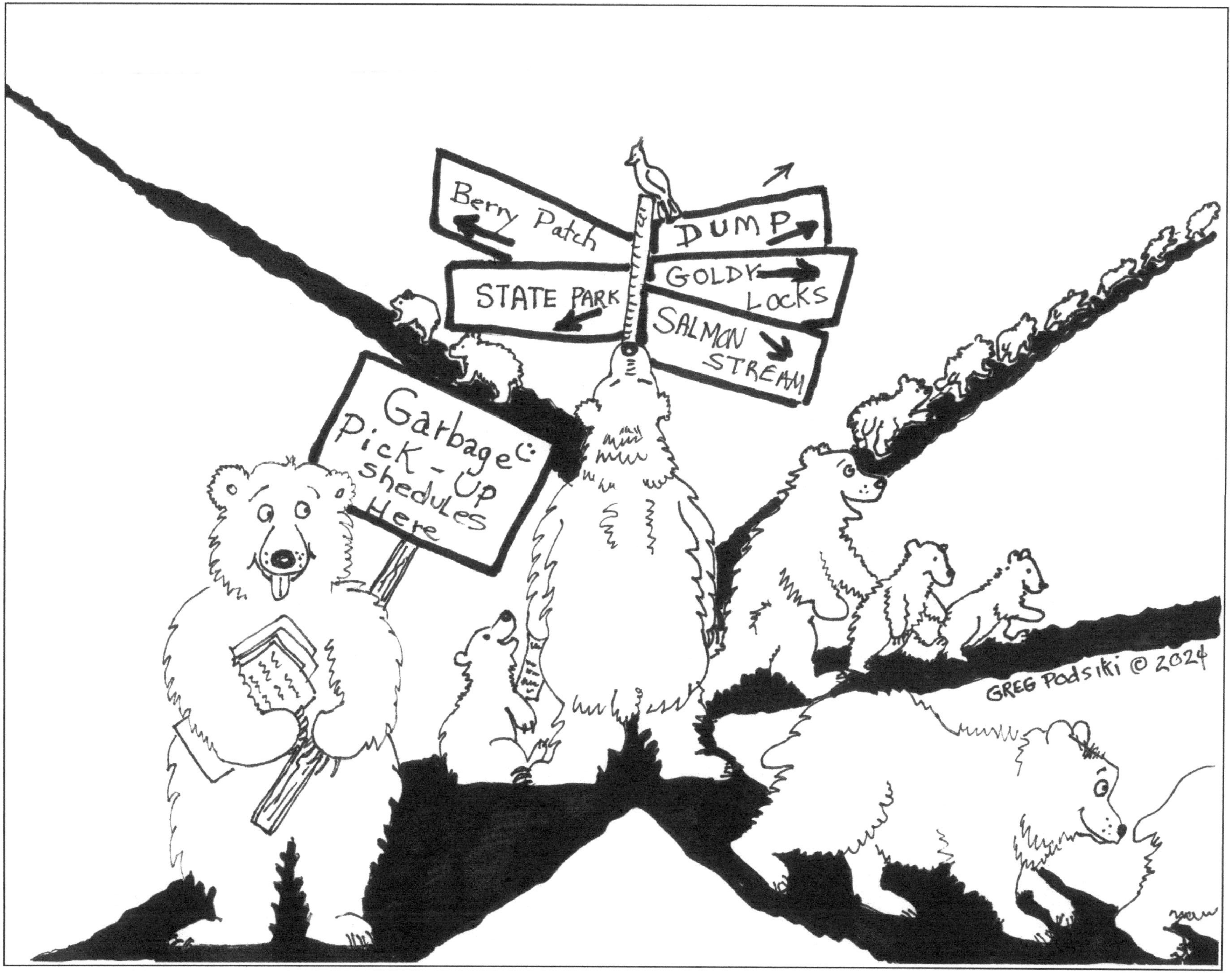
Berry Patch
STATE PARK
DUMP
GOLDY LOCKS
SALMON STREAM
Garbage Pick-Up shedules Here
GREG Podsiki © 2024

The menu

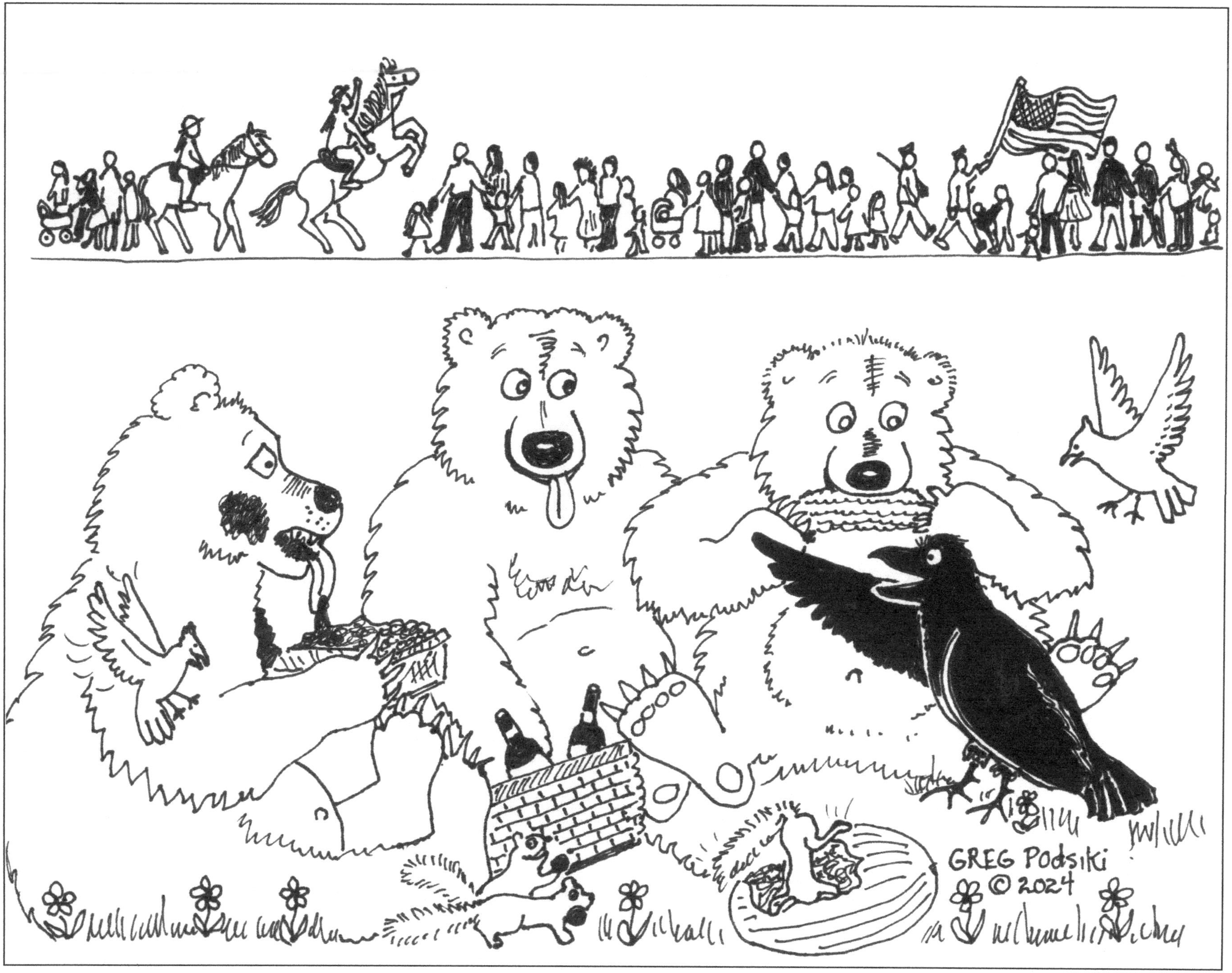
GREG Podsiki
© 2024

Love a parade!

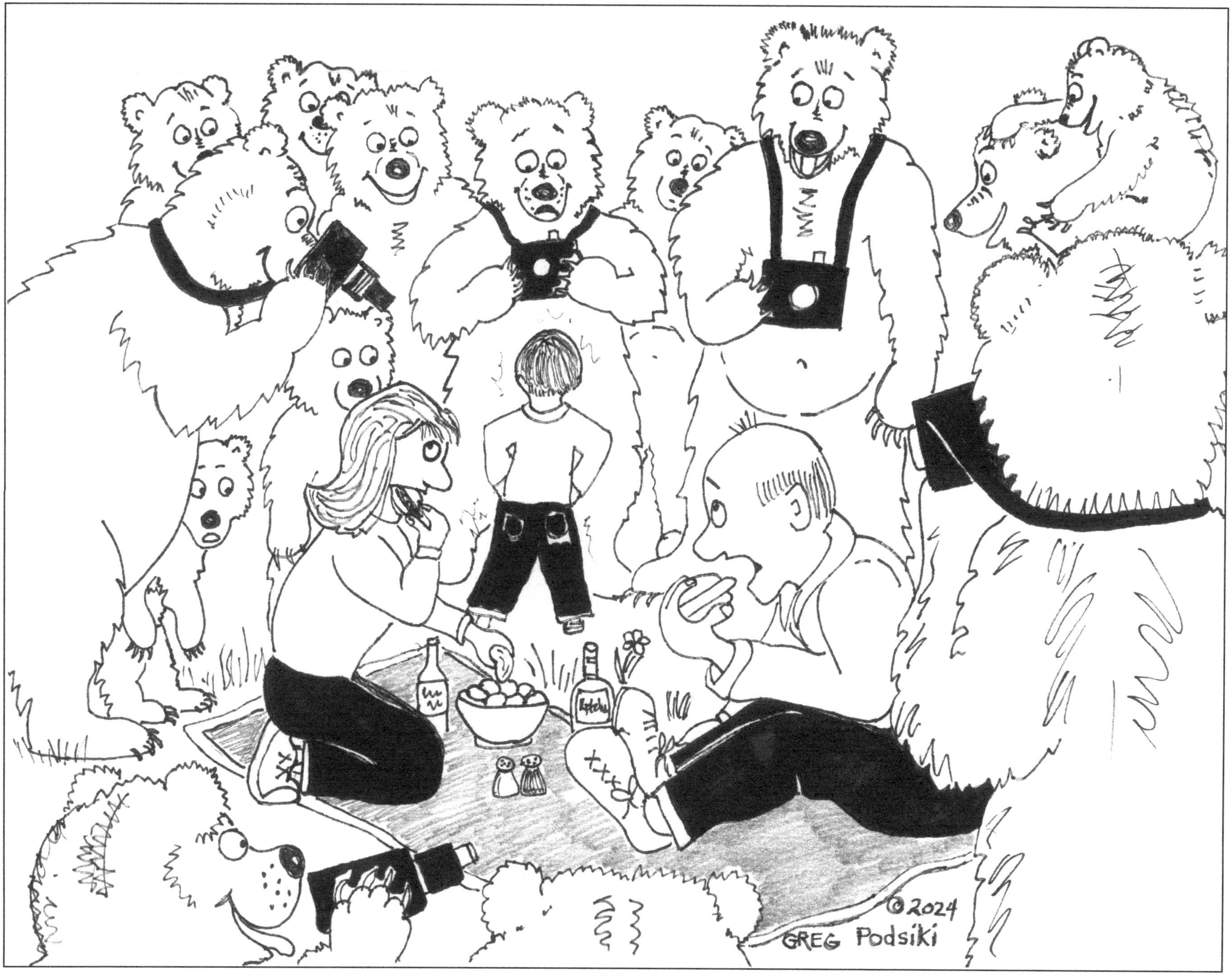
©2024
GREG Podsiki

How embarrassing

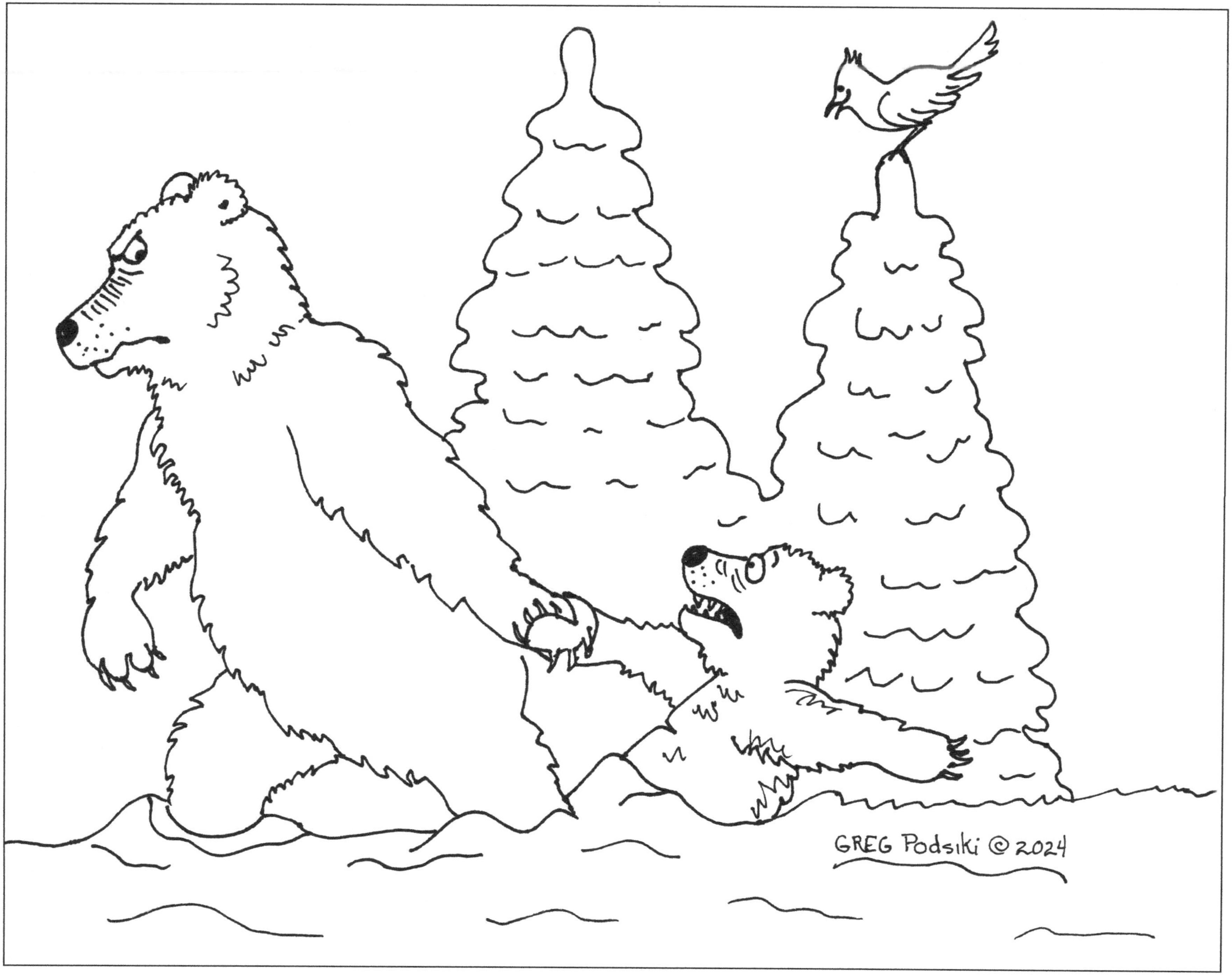
GREG Podsiki © 2024

"I don't want to go to bed yet, mom!"

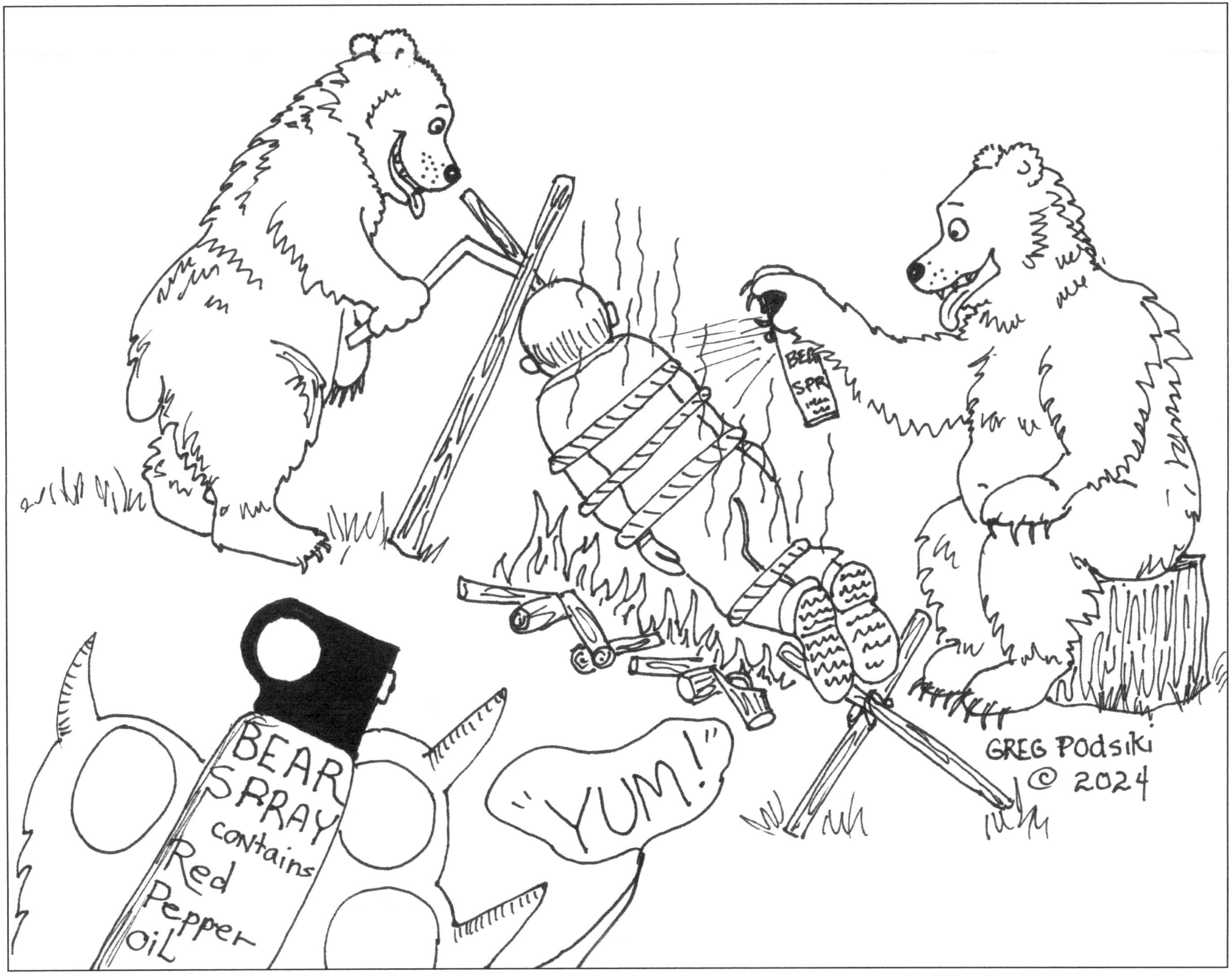
BEAR SPRAY contains Red Pepper oiL
"YUM!"
GREG PODSIKI © 2024

"Let's spice him up!"

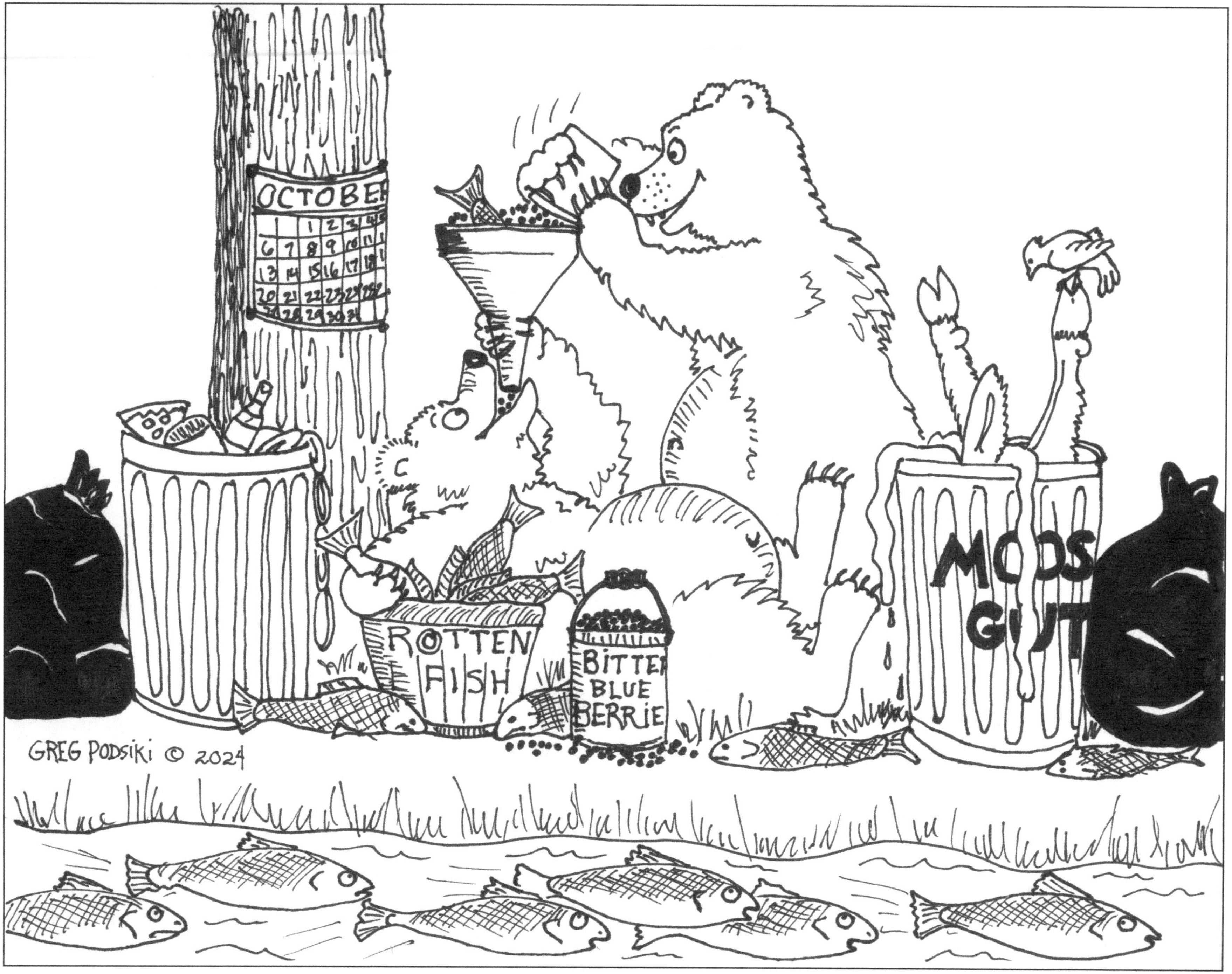
OCTOBER
ROTTEN FISH
BITTER BLUE BERRIE
MOOS GUT
GREG PODSIKI © 2024

Desperate times (winter is just around the corner)

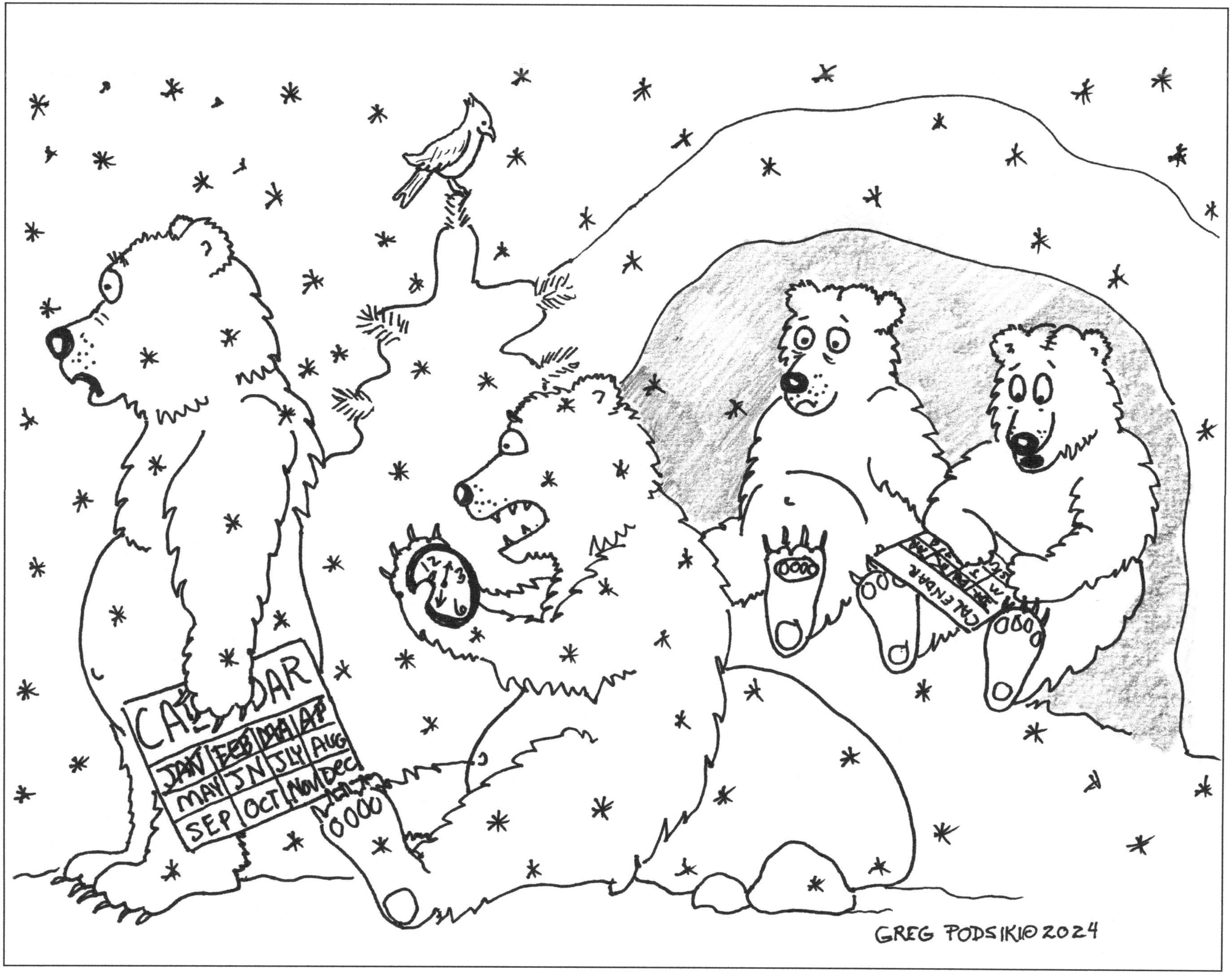
CALENDAR
JAN FEB MAR AP
MAY JN JLY AUG
SEP OCT NOV DEC
CALENDAR
GREG PODSIKI© 2024

"You've GOT TO BE KIDDING!! It's MAY!"

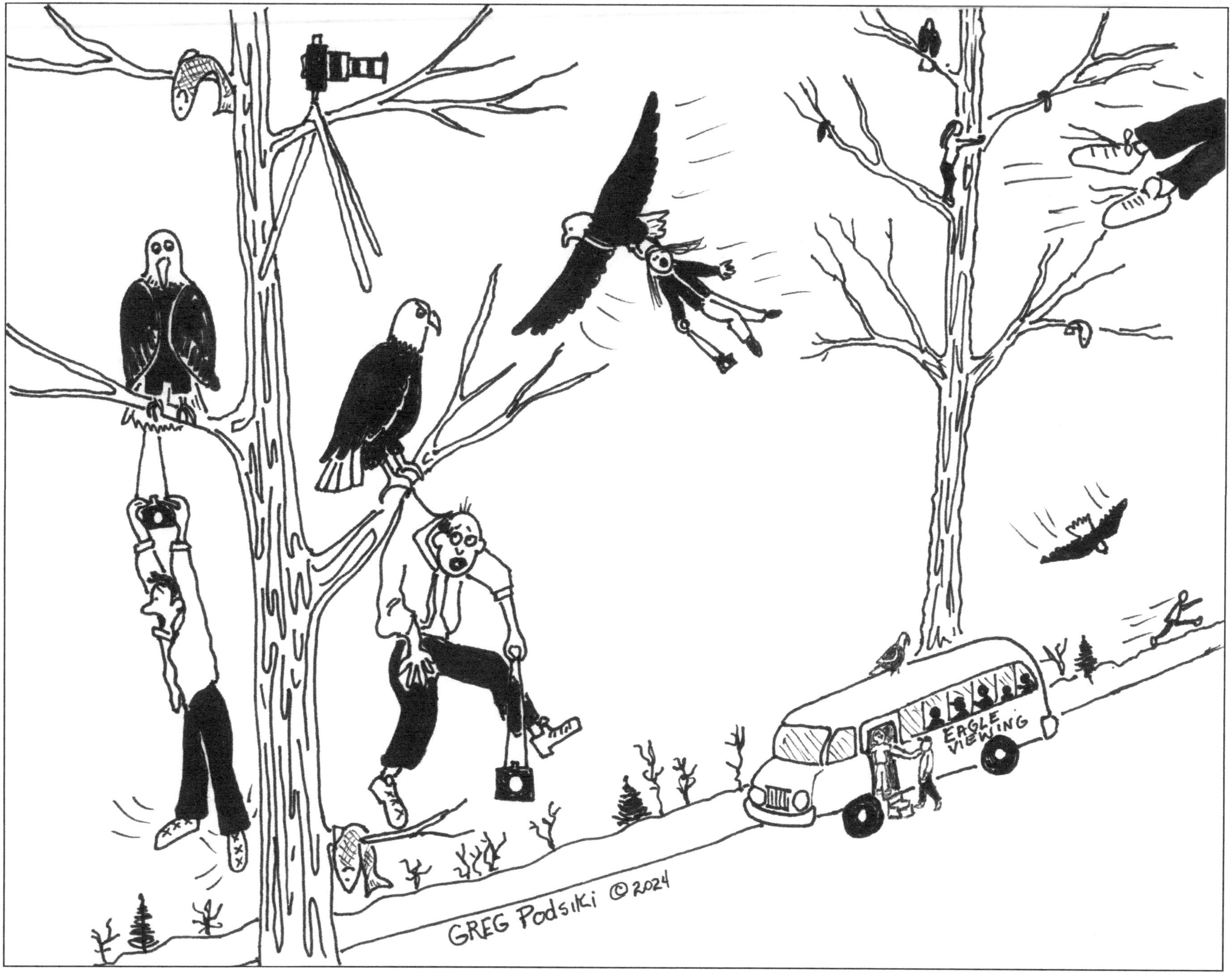
EAGLE VIEWING
GREG Podsiki ©2024

Never wiggle like a salmon!

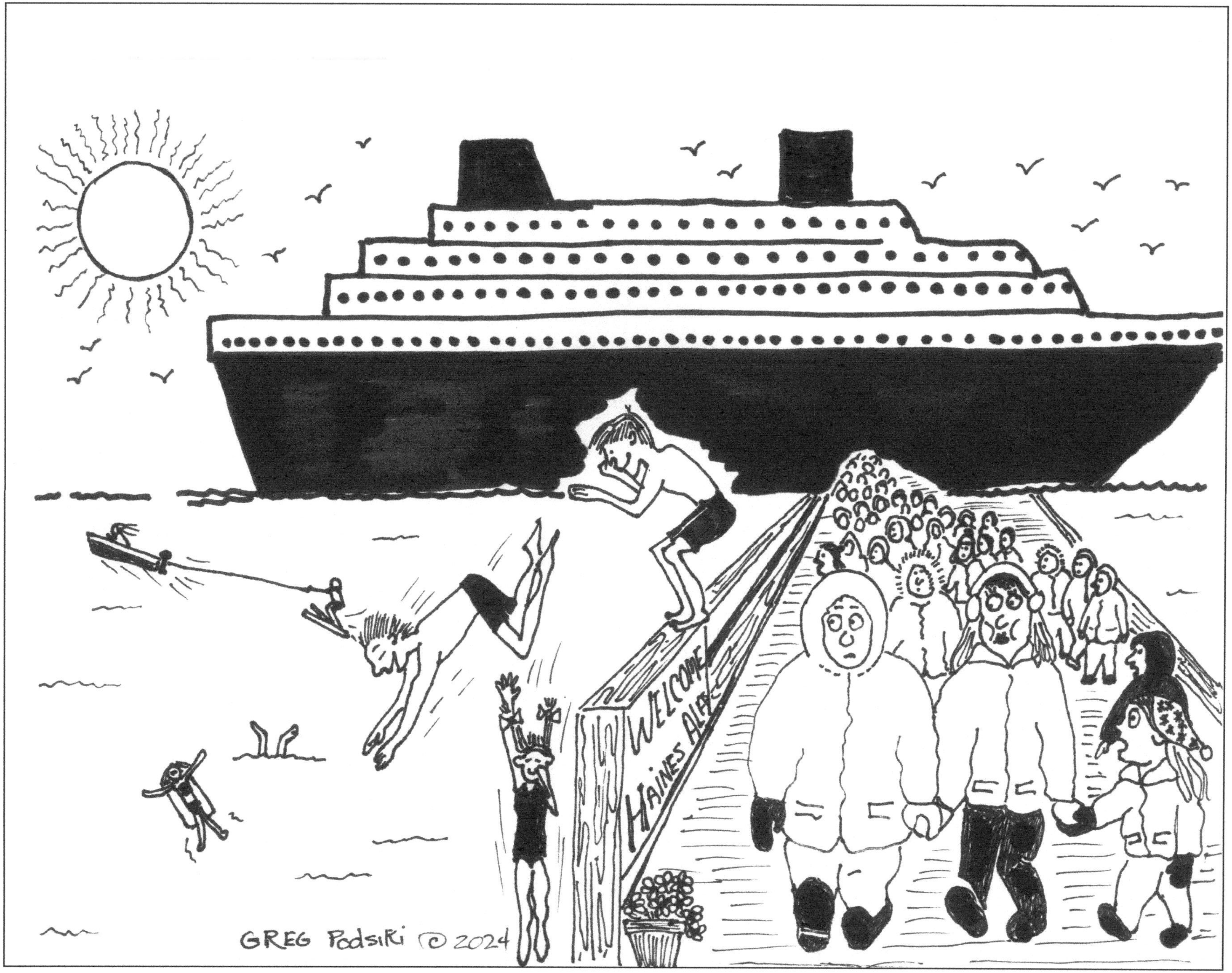
WELCOME
HAINES ALA
GREG Podsiki © 2024

60°F in Alaska!! Yippee!!

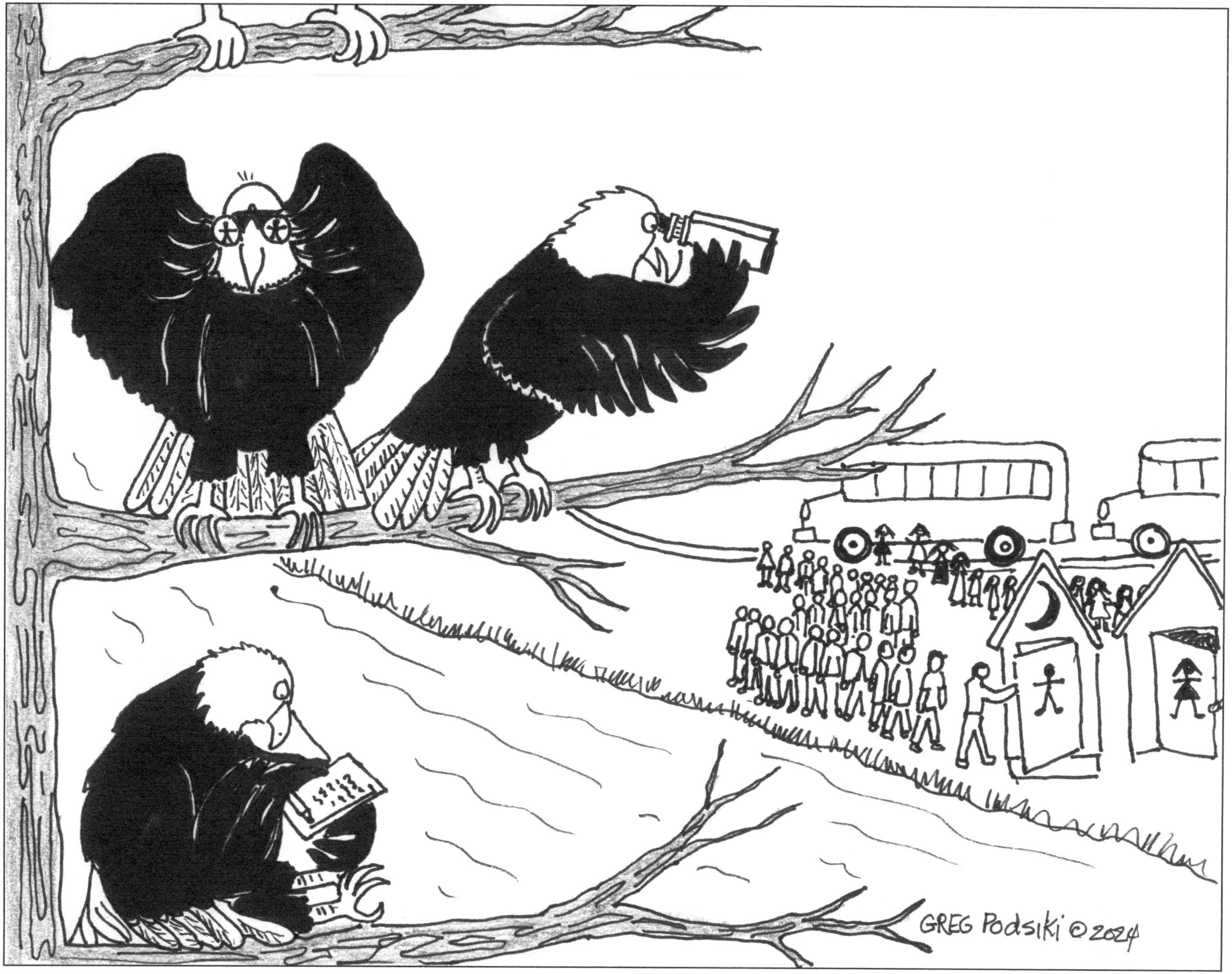
GREG Podsiki © 2024

"I count 41 females and 38 males"

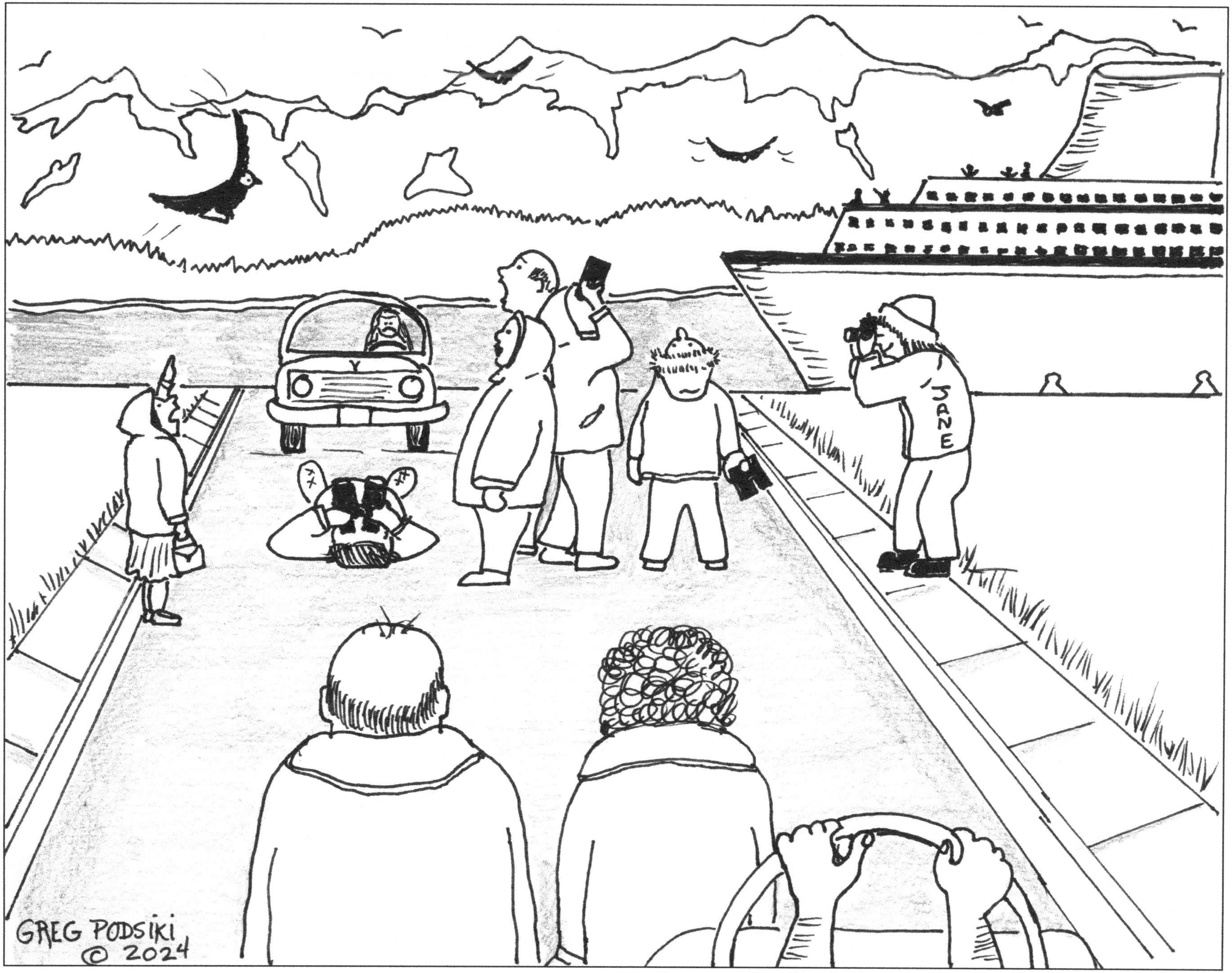
JANE
GREG PODSIKI
© 2024

Attention tourists! Be like Jane!

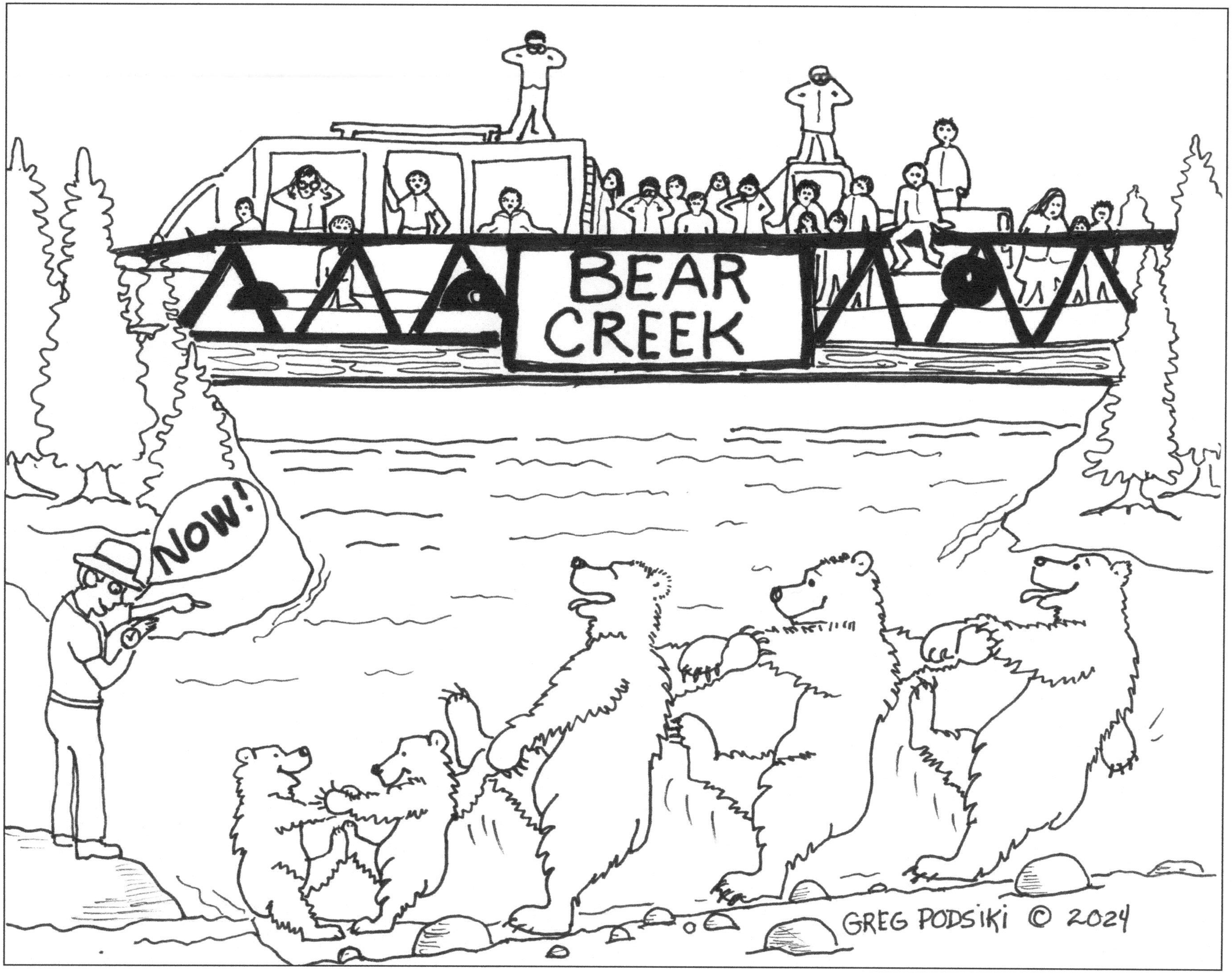
BEAR CREEK
Now!
GREG PODSIKI © 2024

A one, and a two, and a three...

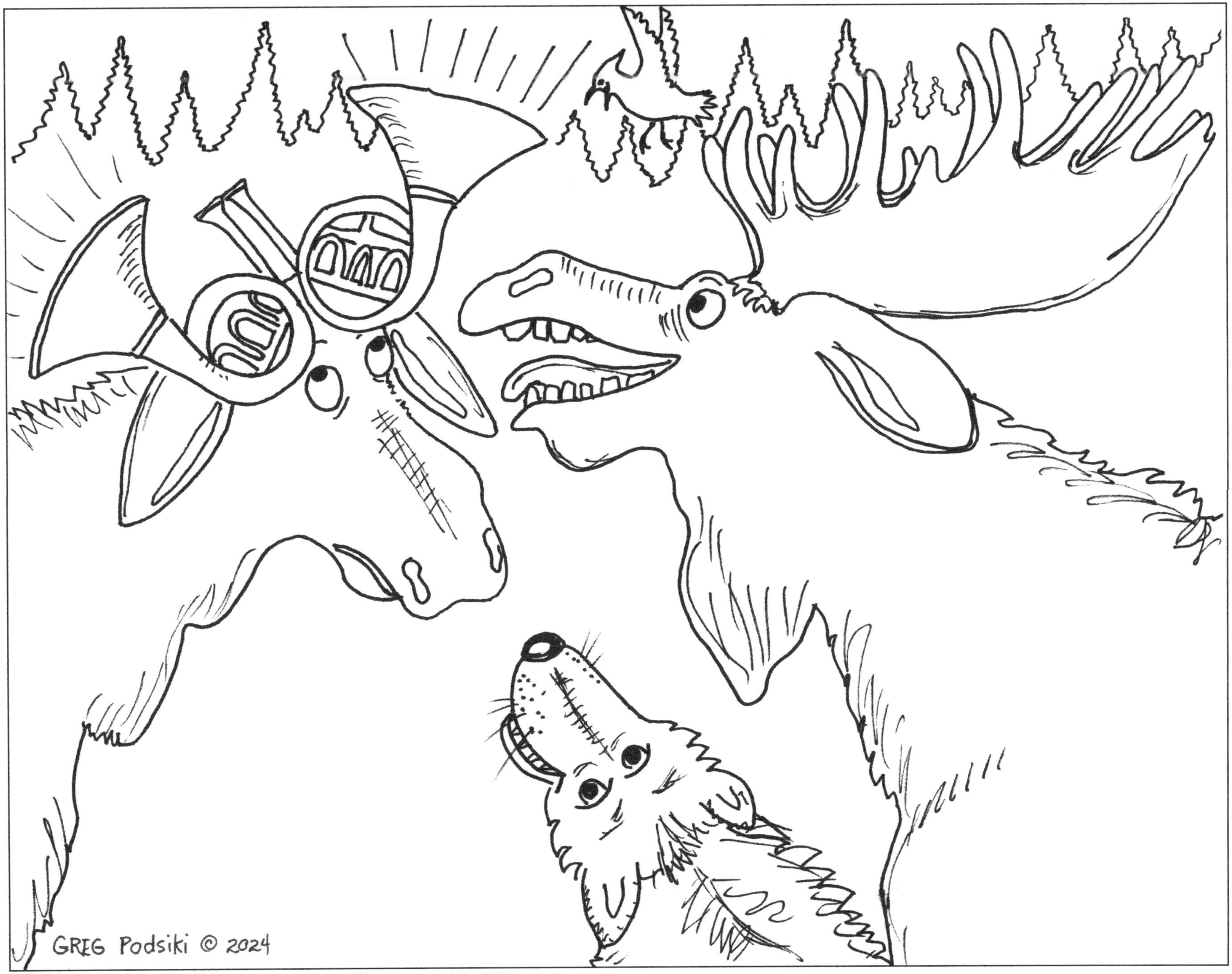
GREG Podsiki © 2024

Genetics! (Moose don't have horns. They have antlers)

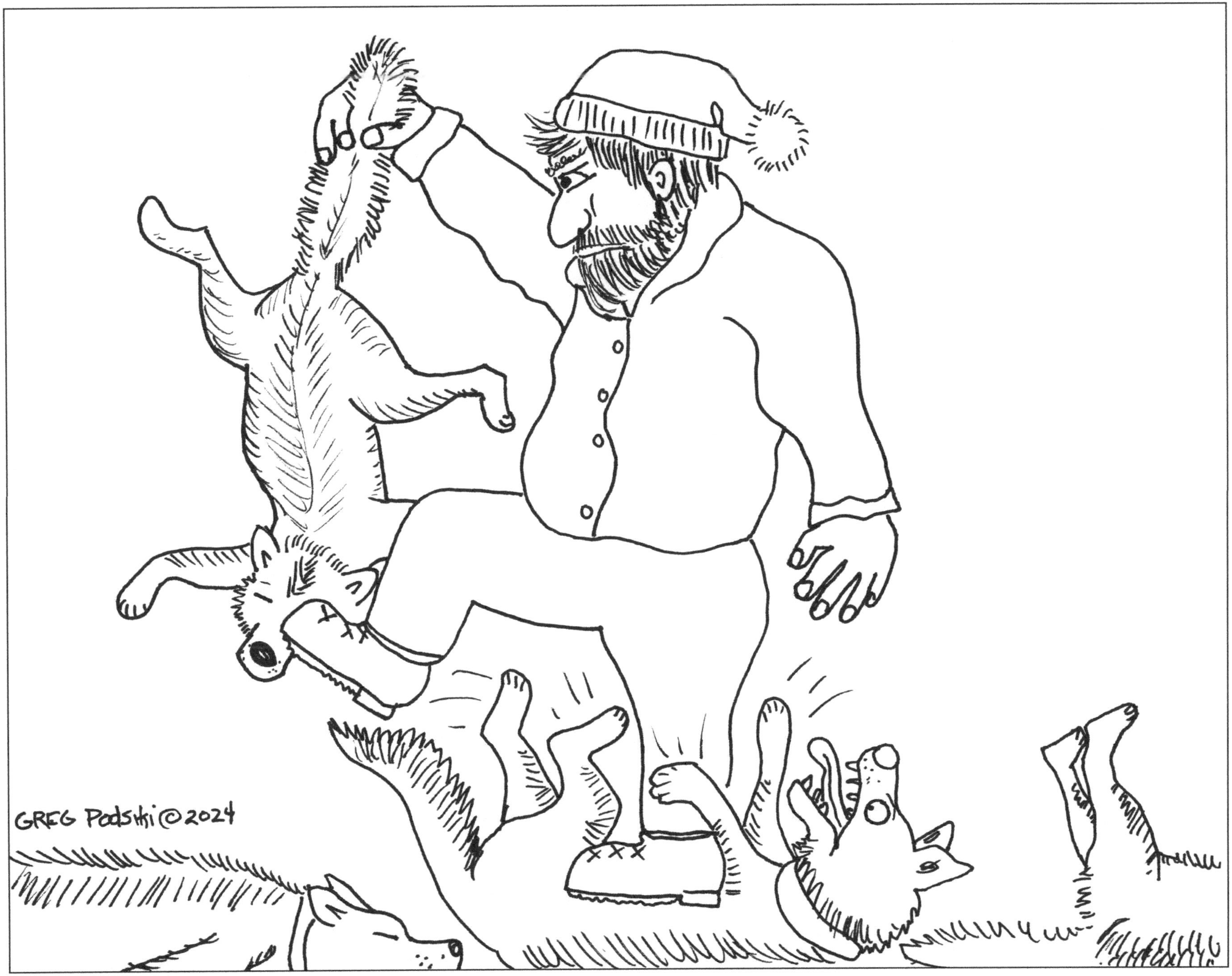
GREG Podski©2024

Dog mushing (not really. “dog mushing” is a term used for dog sledding: “mush you huskies”)

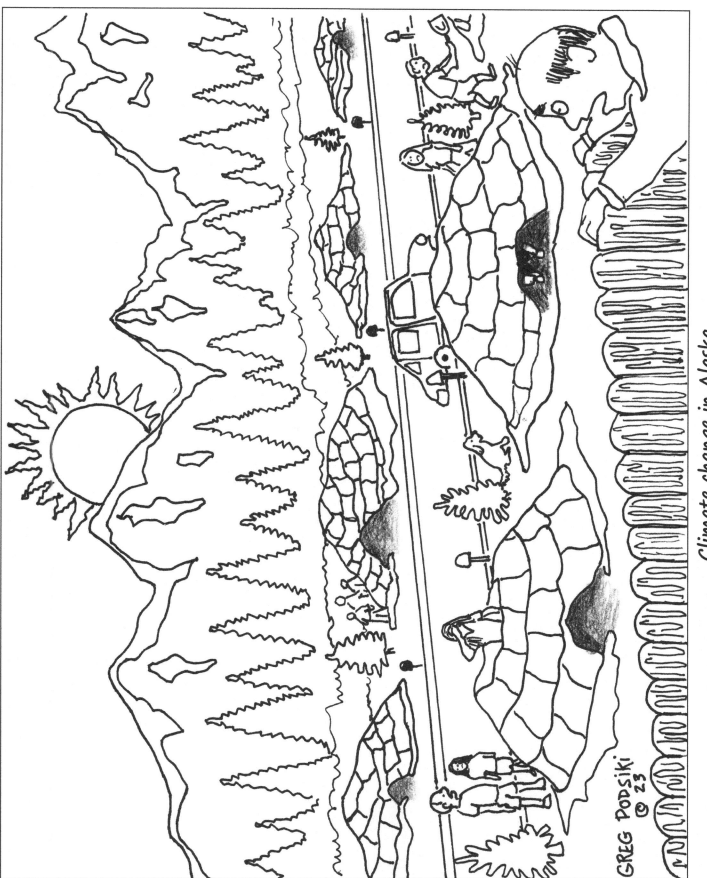

Climate change in Alaska

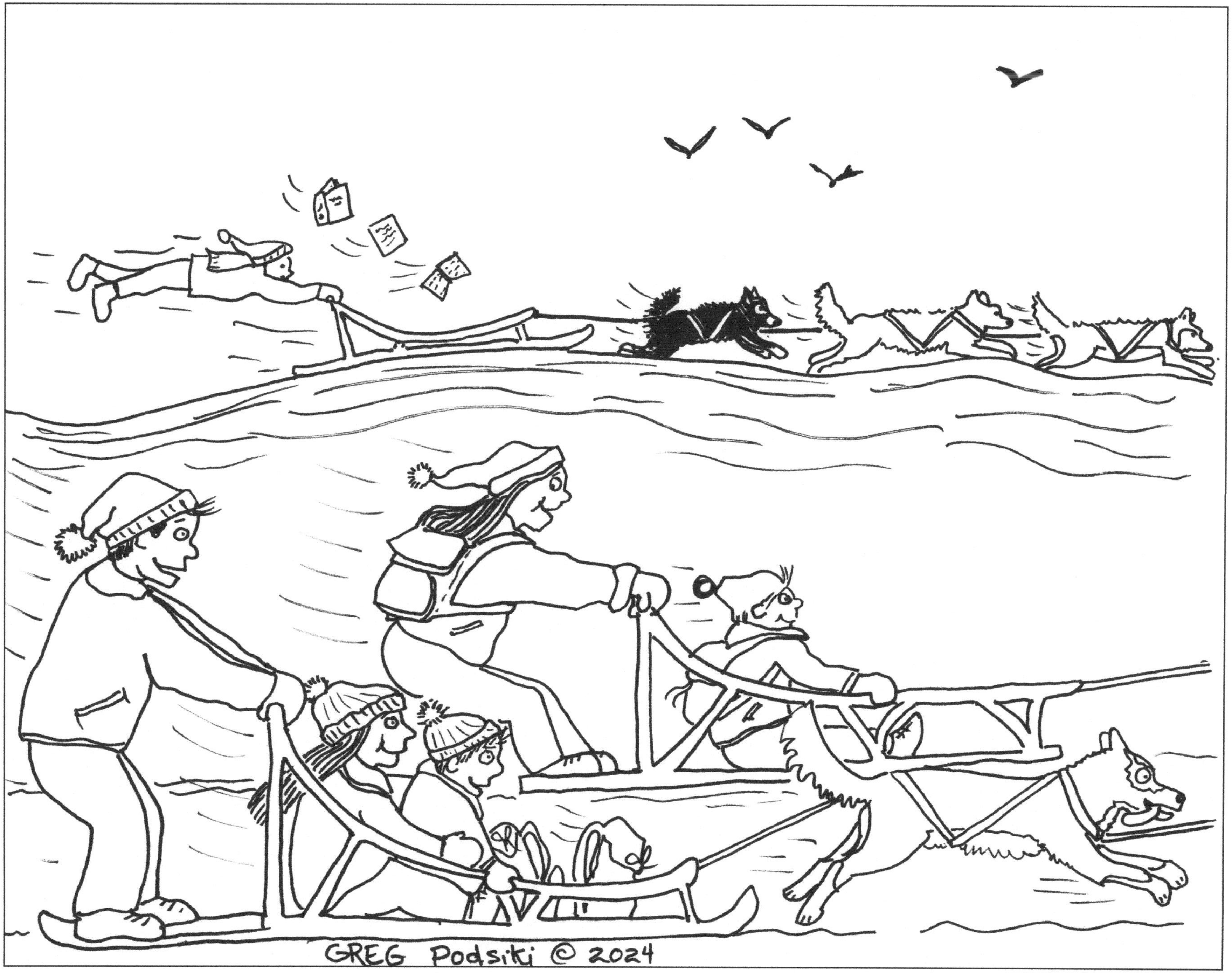
GREG Podsiki © 2024

How Alaskan kids get to school (100 years ago)

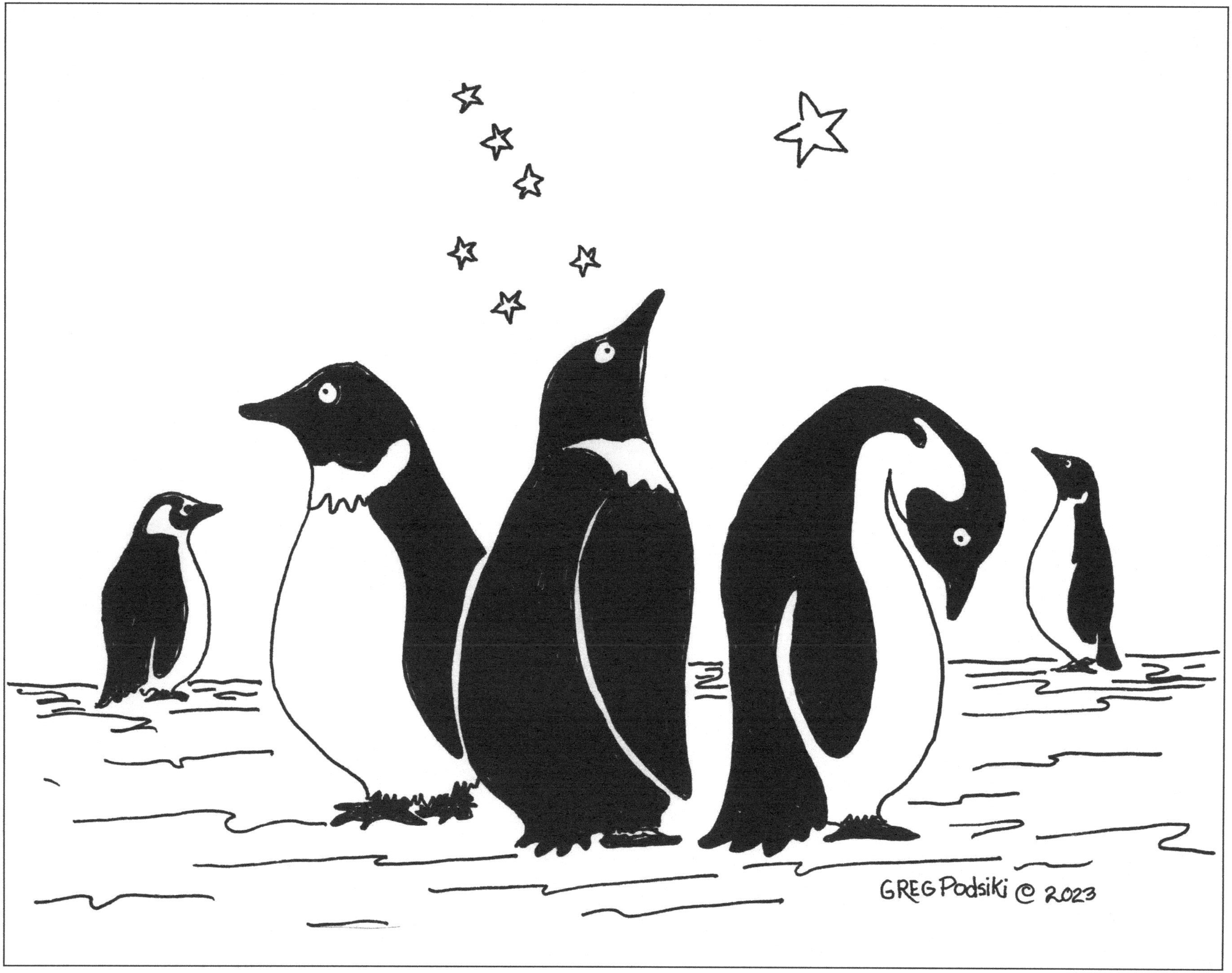
GREG Podsiki © 2023

Lost souls in Alaska (we do not have penguins – the polar bears eat them all)

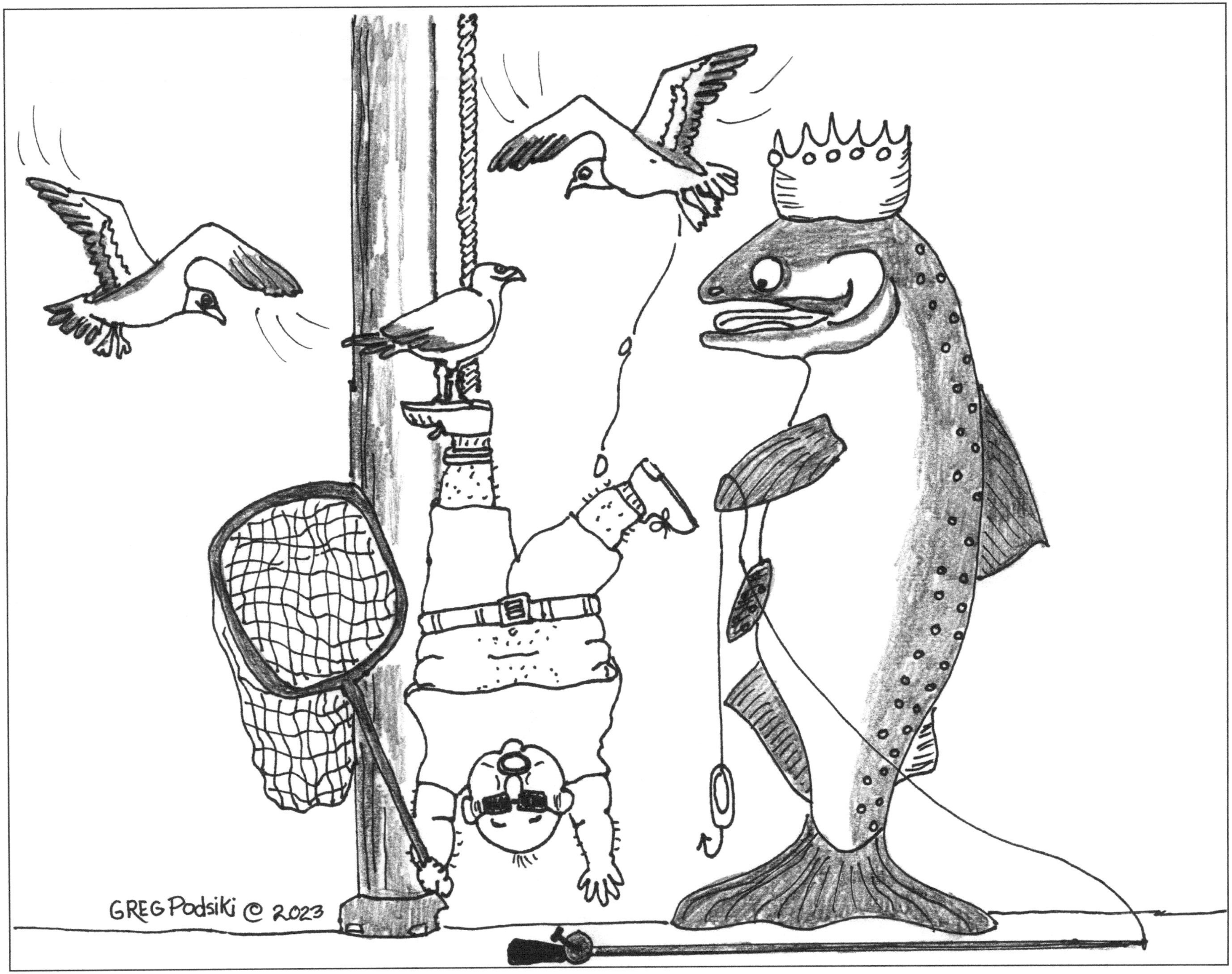
GREG Podsiki © 2023

The winner of the king salmon derby

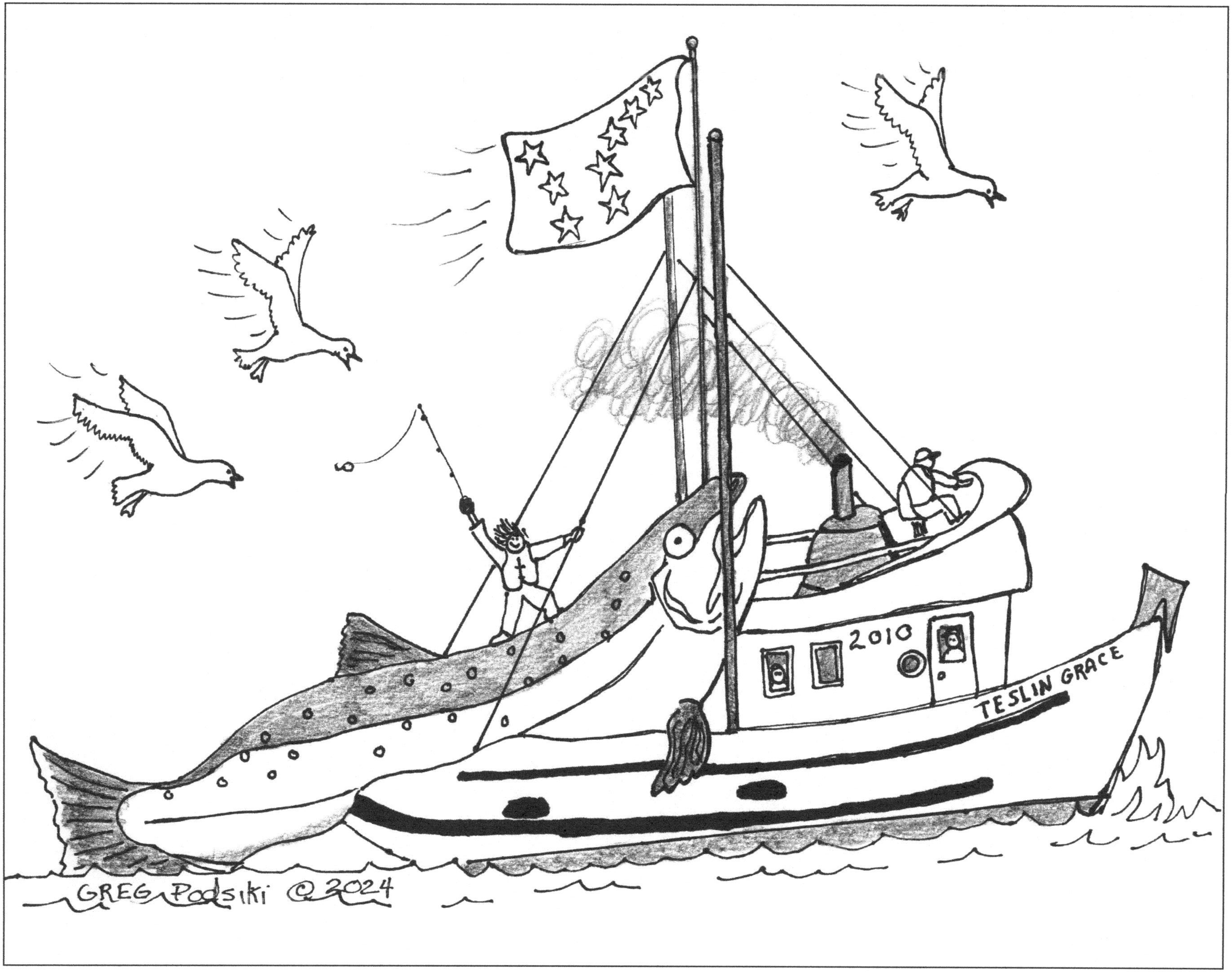

2010
TESLIN GRACE
GREG Podsiki © 2024

Limited out!

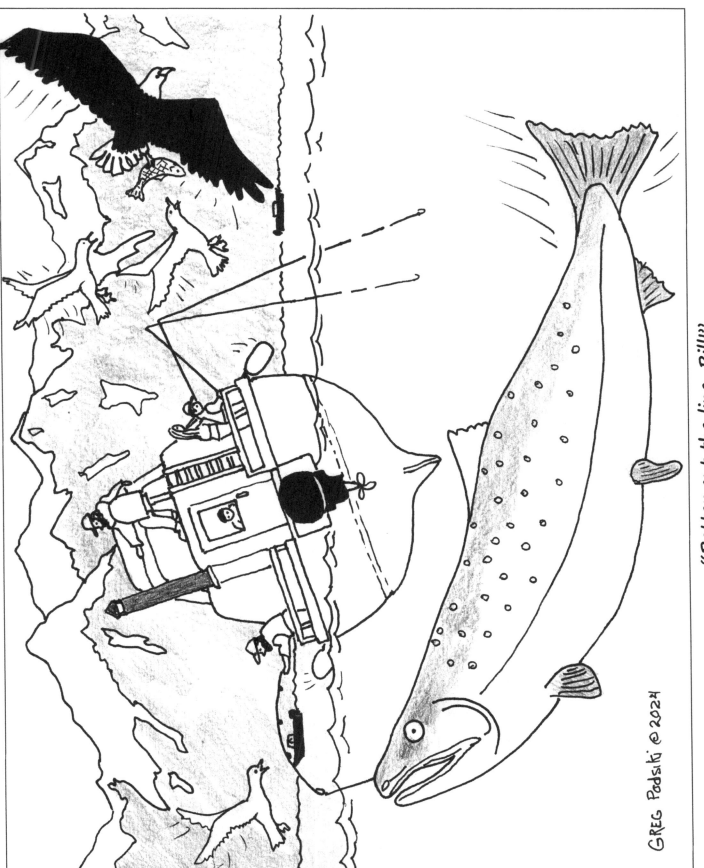

"Better cut the line, Bill!"

GREG Podski © 2024

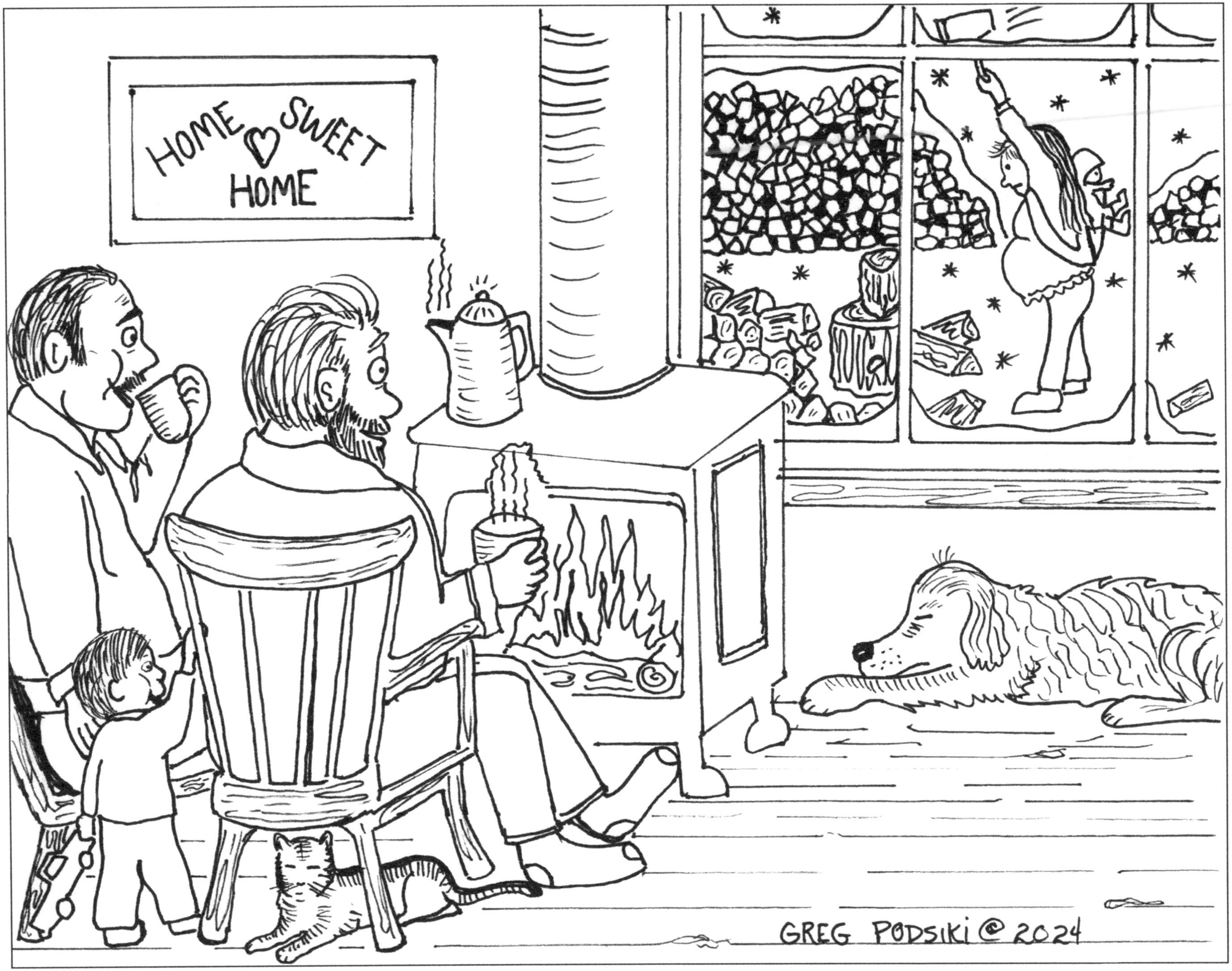
HOME ♡ SWEET HOME
GREG PODSIKI © 2024

"Does she have a sister?"

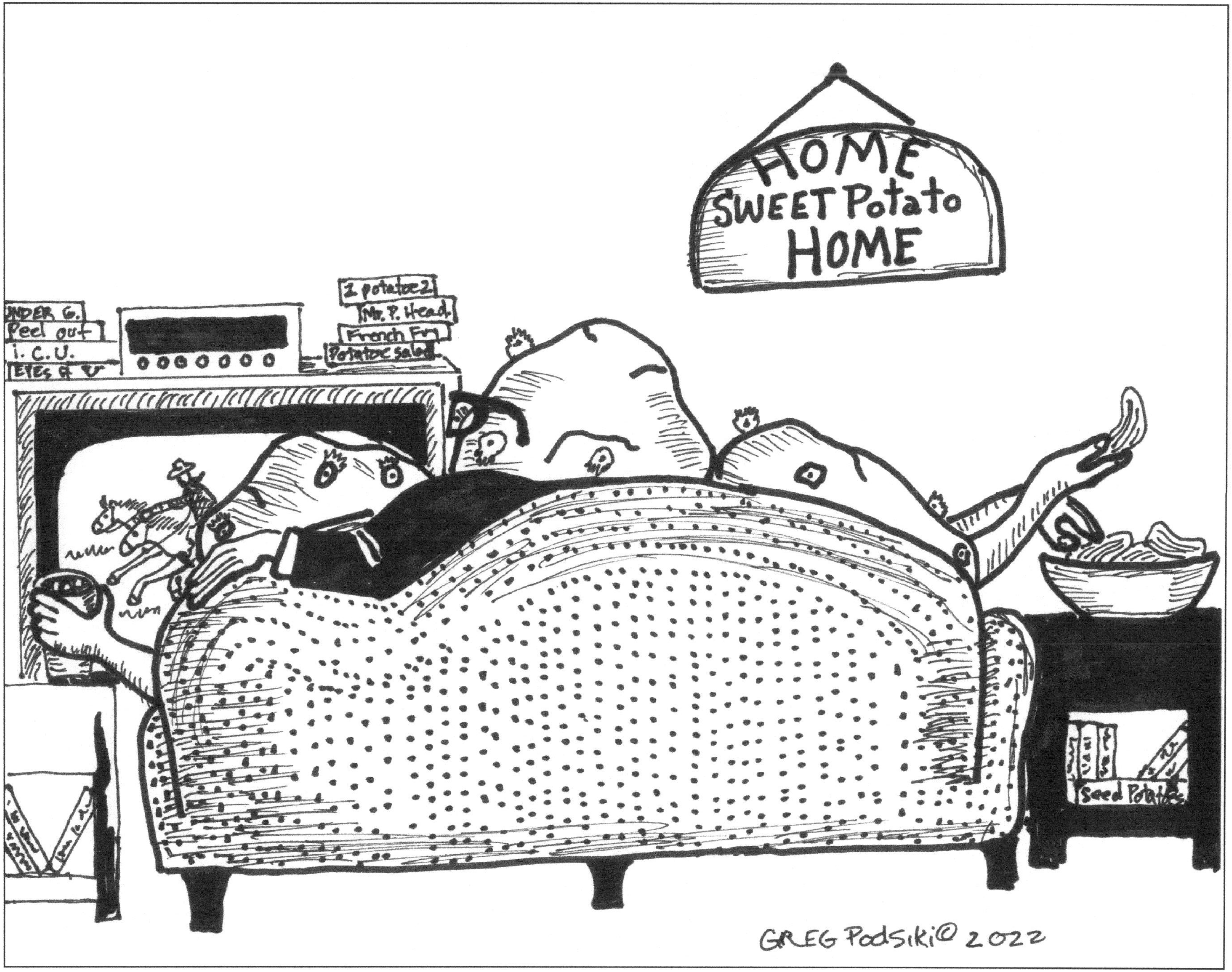
HOME
SWEET Potato
HOME
UNDER G.
Peel out
i. C.U.
EYES of
1 potatoe 2
Mr. P. Head
French Fry
Potatoe salad
Seed Potatoes
GREG Podsiki© 2022

Alaskans in those long winters

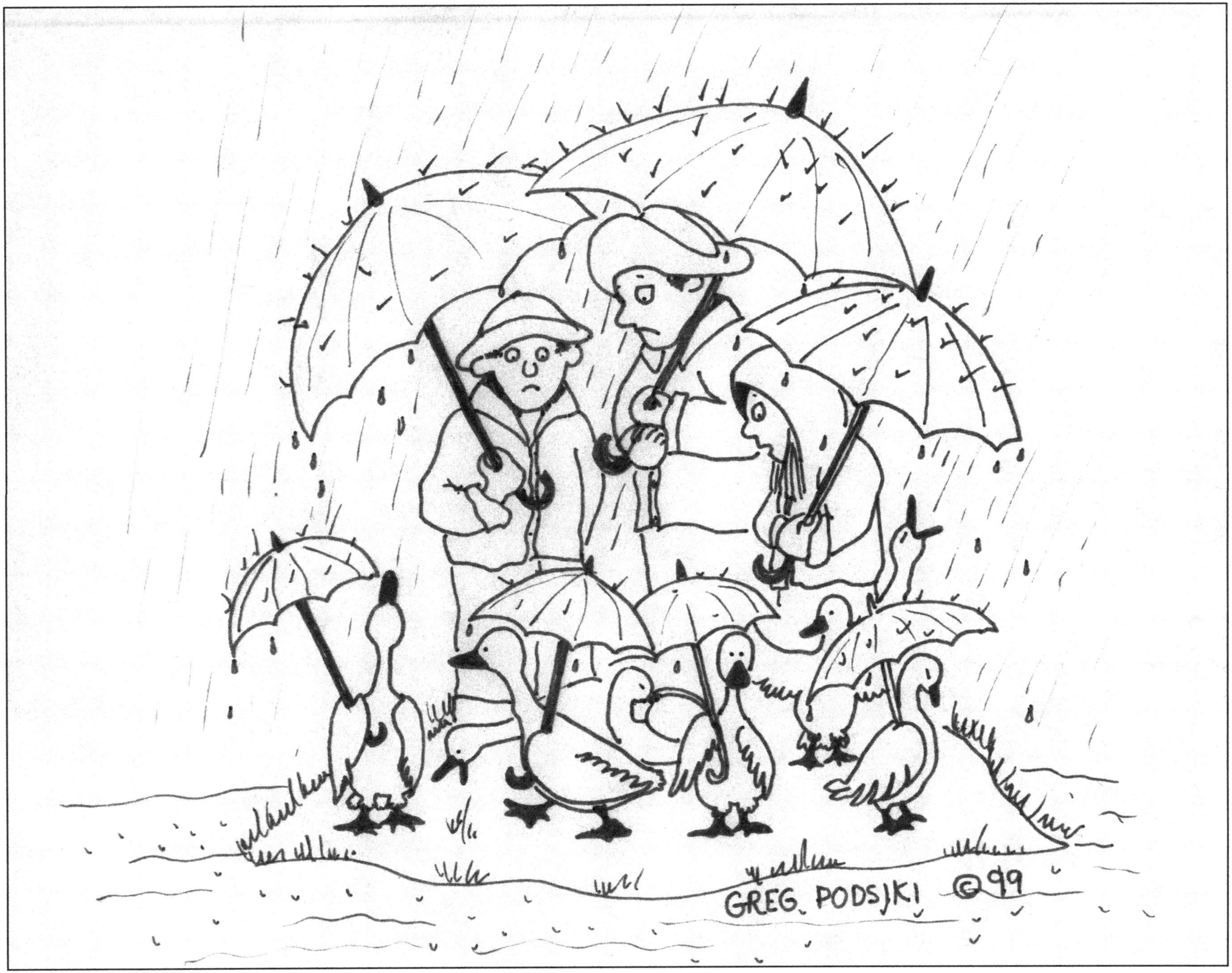
GREG. PODSJKI ©99

Even the ducks are taking cover

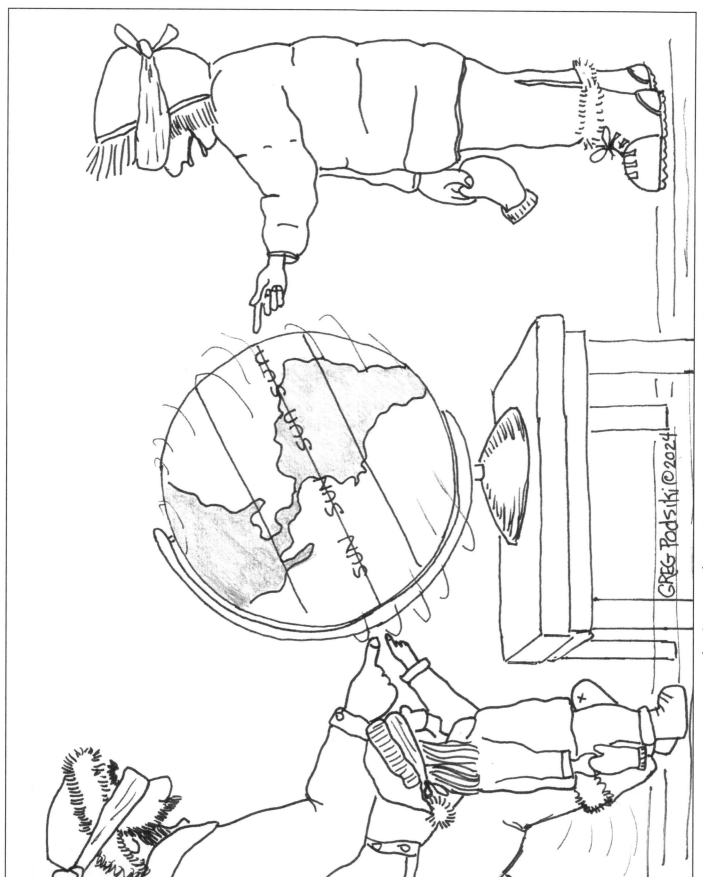

Alaskans planning a winter vacation destination

GREG Podsiki ©2024

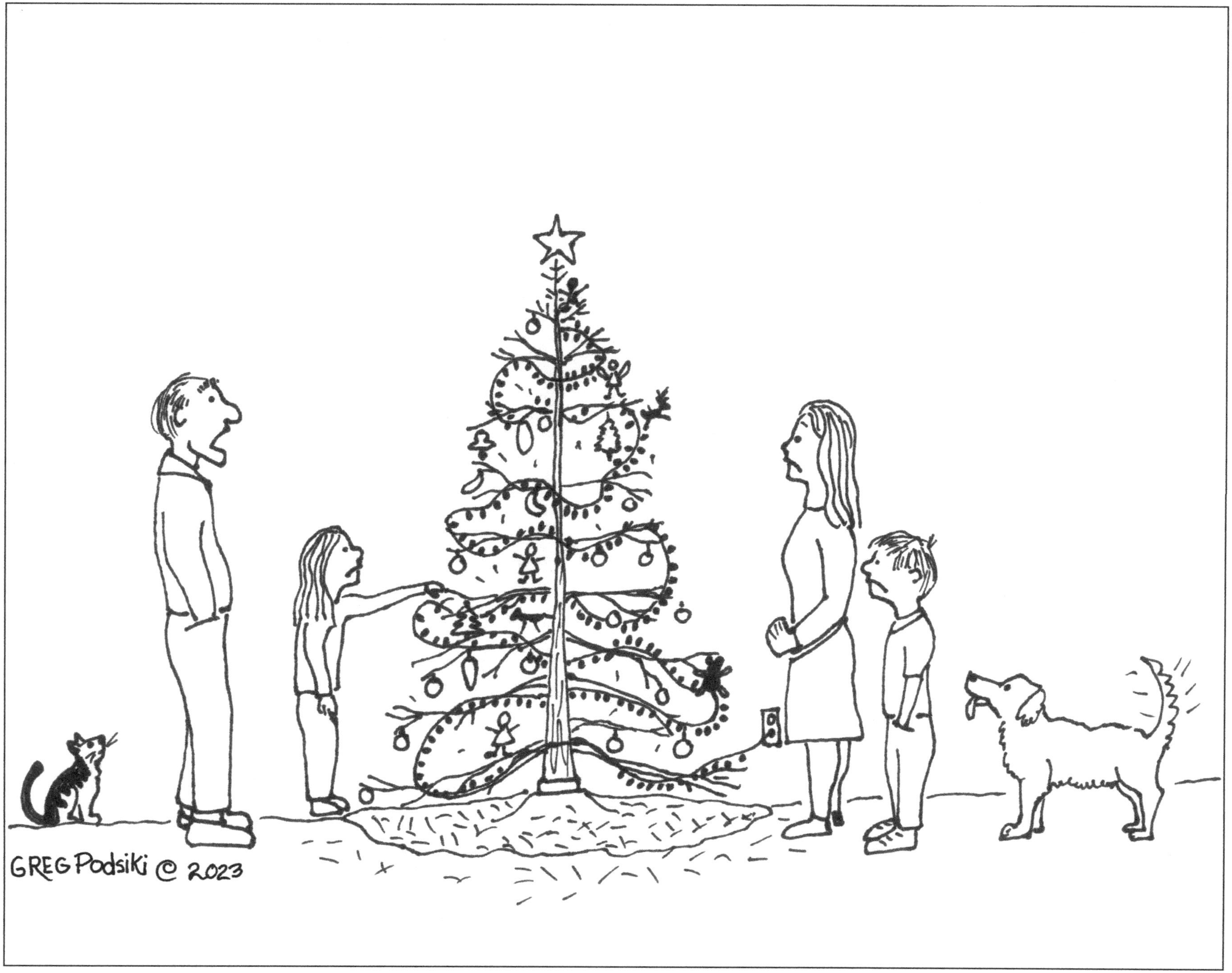
GREG Podsiki © 2023

"Honey... time to put up the Easter decorations"

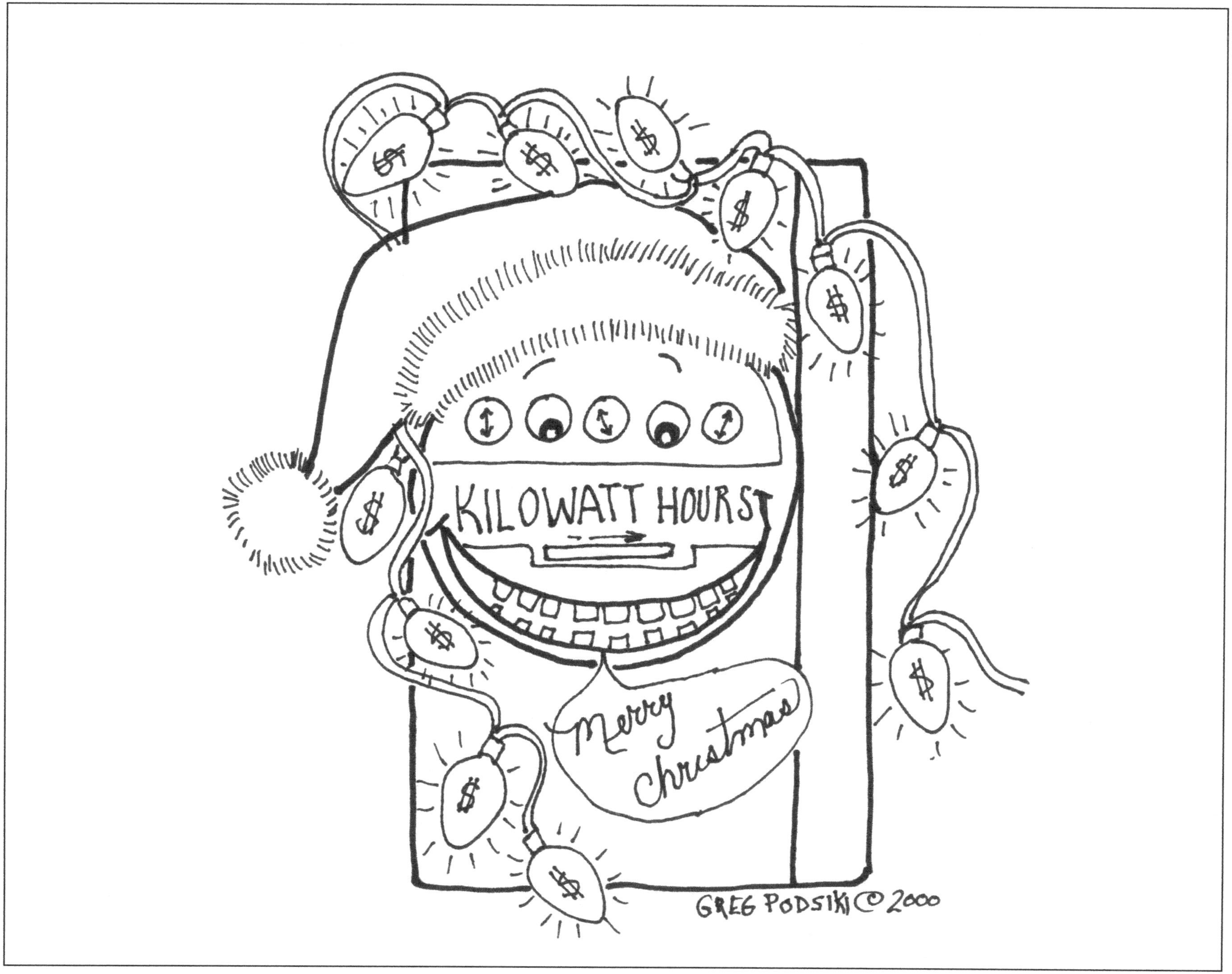
KILOWATT HOURS
Merry Christmas
GREG PODSIKI © 2000

It's that time of the year – ching, ching!

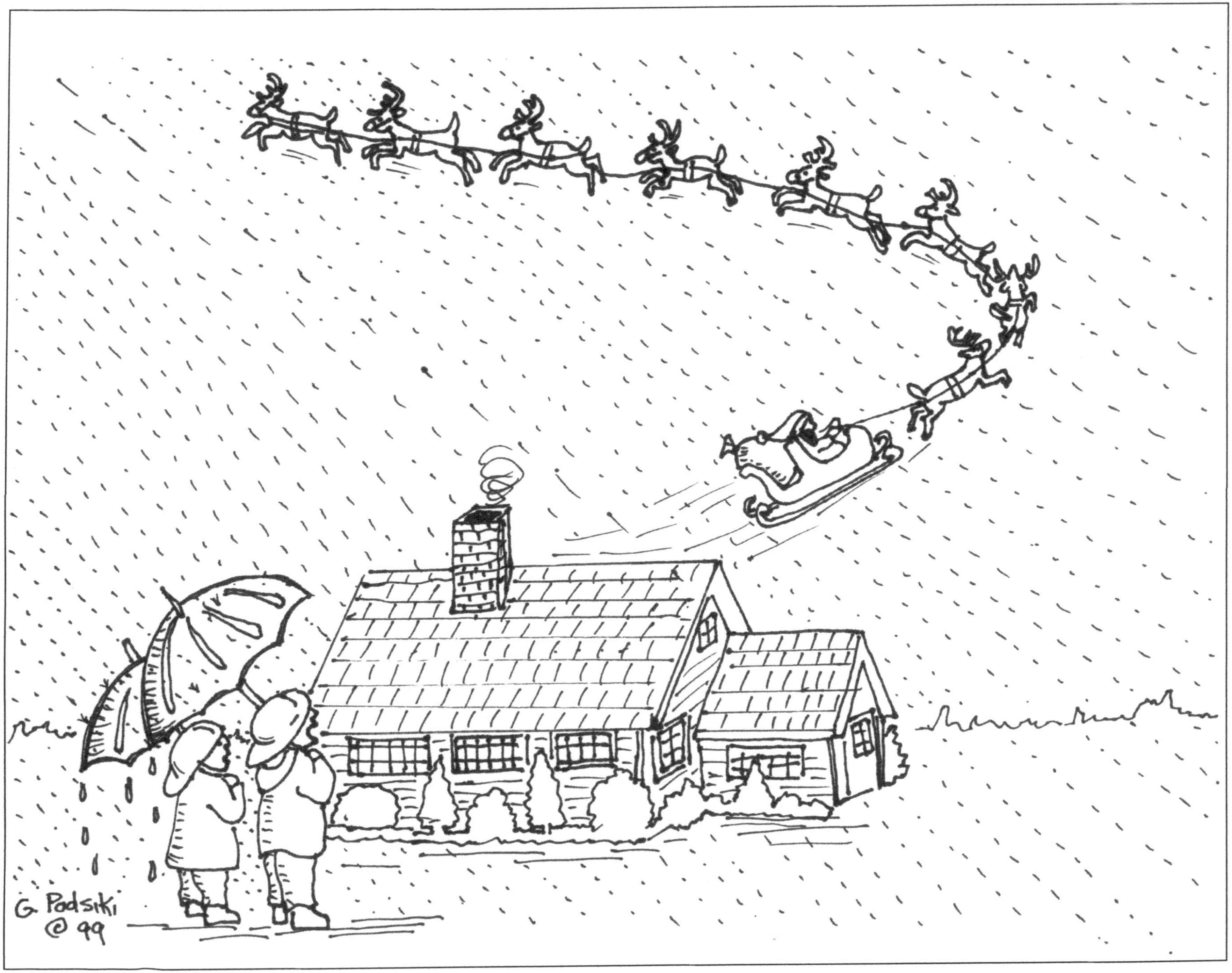
G. Podsiki
@ 99

It's a good thing Santa uses "rain" deer

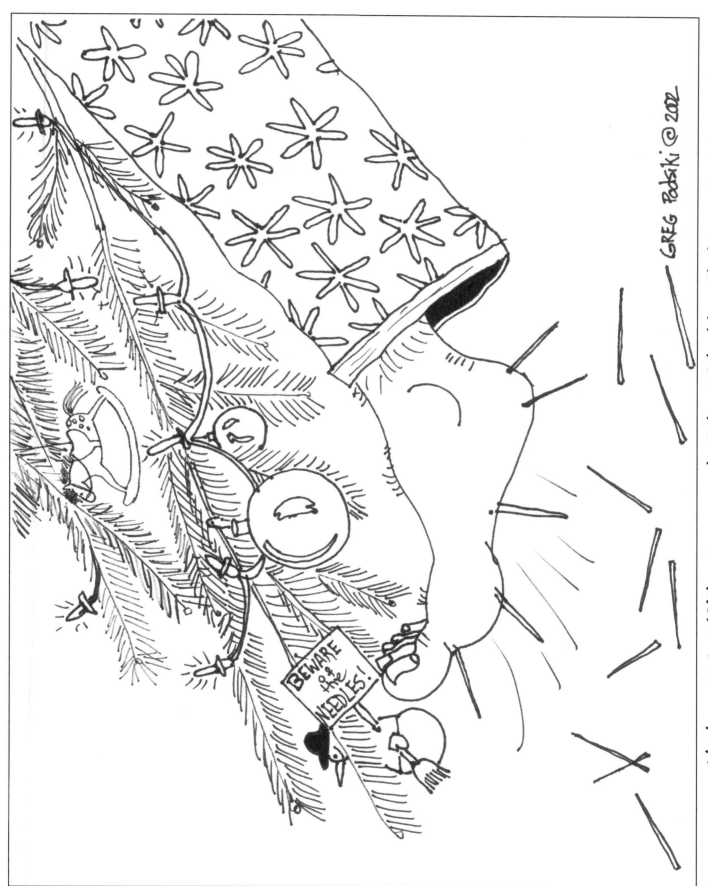

Alaskan cactus (Sitka spruce make "sharp" looking Christmas trees)

GREG Podsiki © 2022

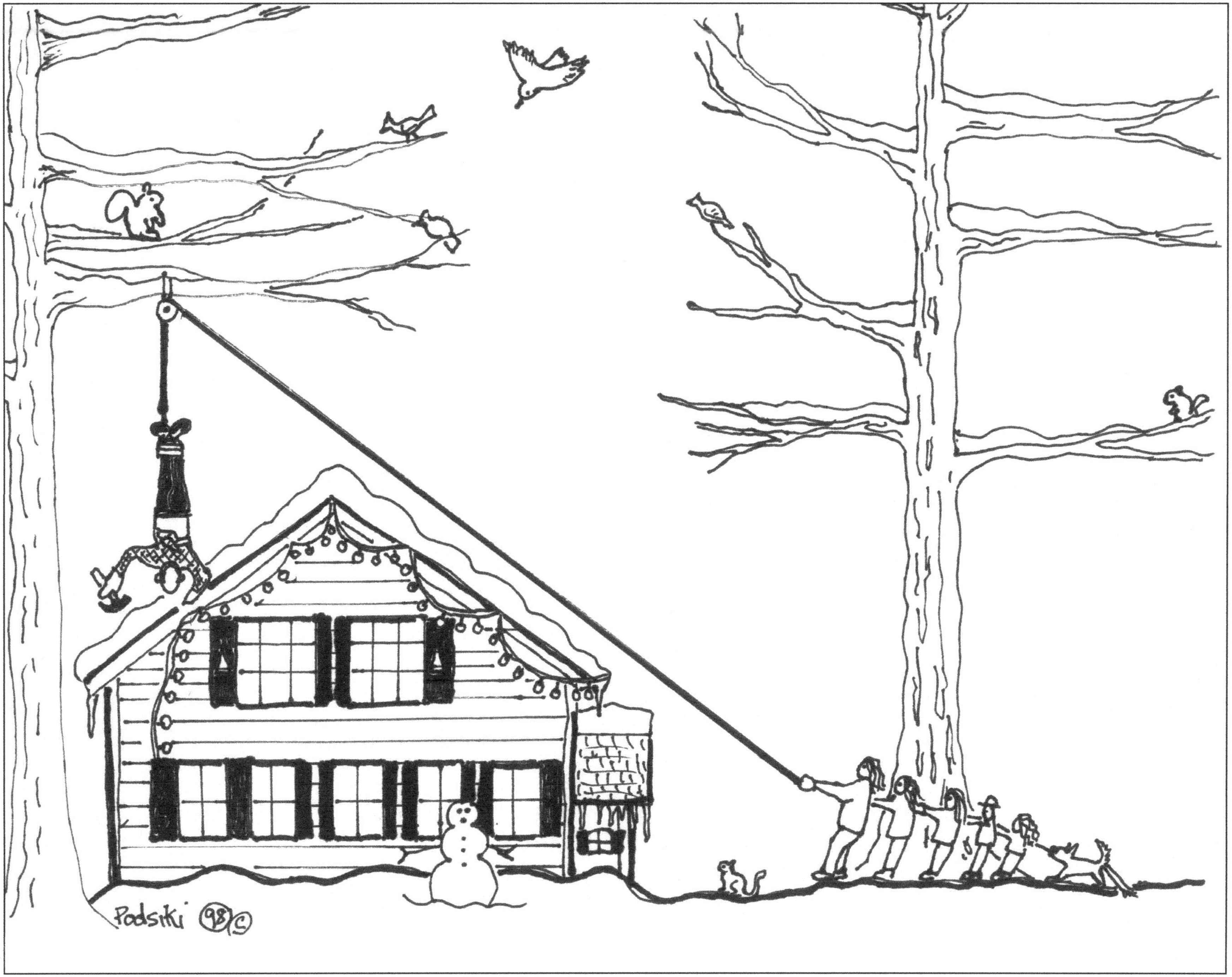
Podsiki 98 C

Where there's a will, there's a way

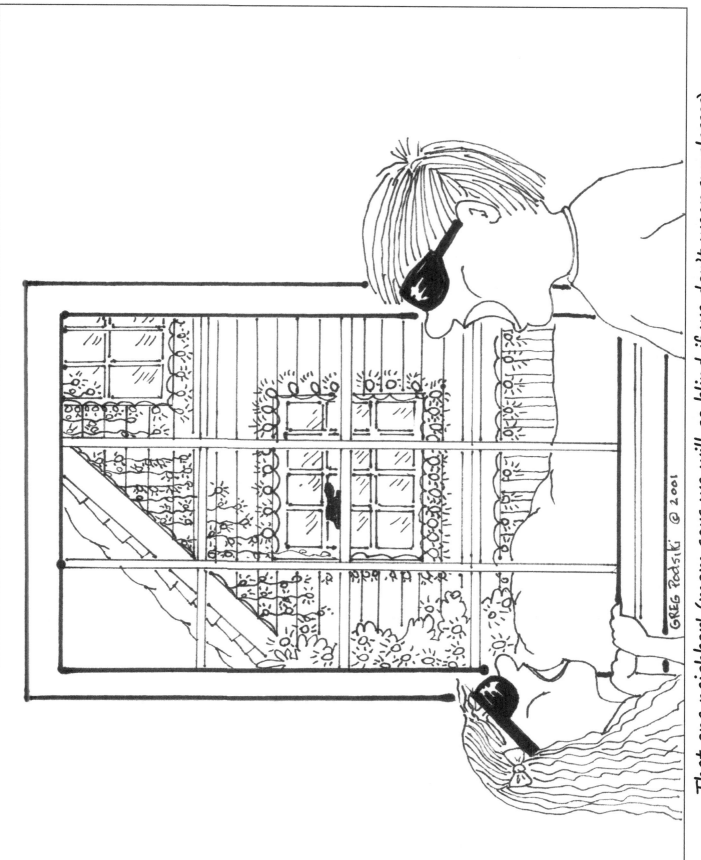

That one neighbor! (mom says we will go blind if we don't wear sunglasses)

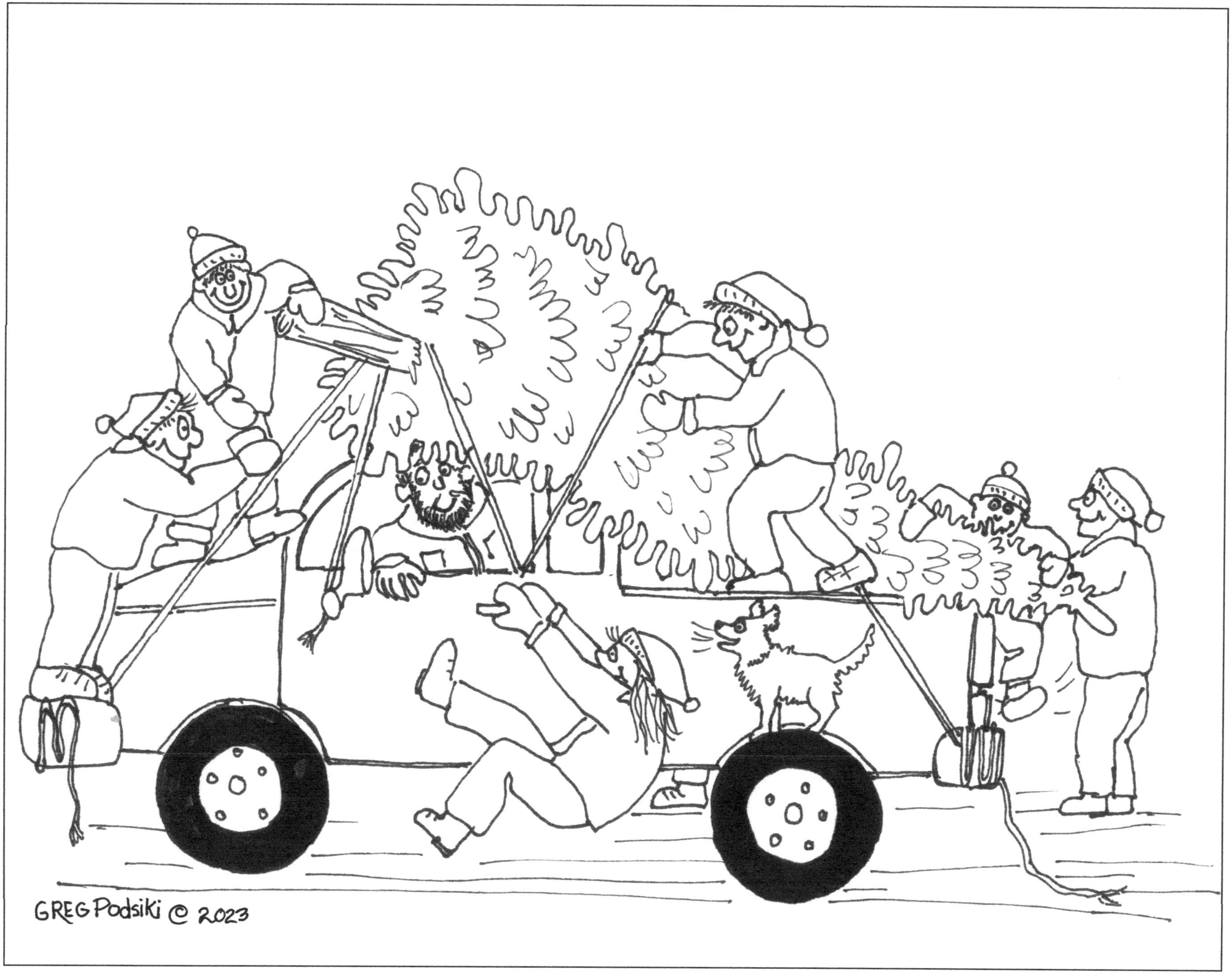
GREG Podsiki © 2023

Too much help

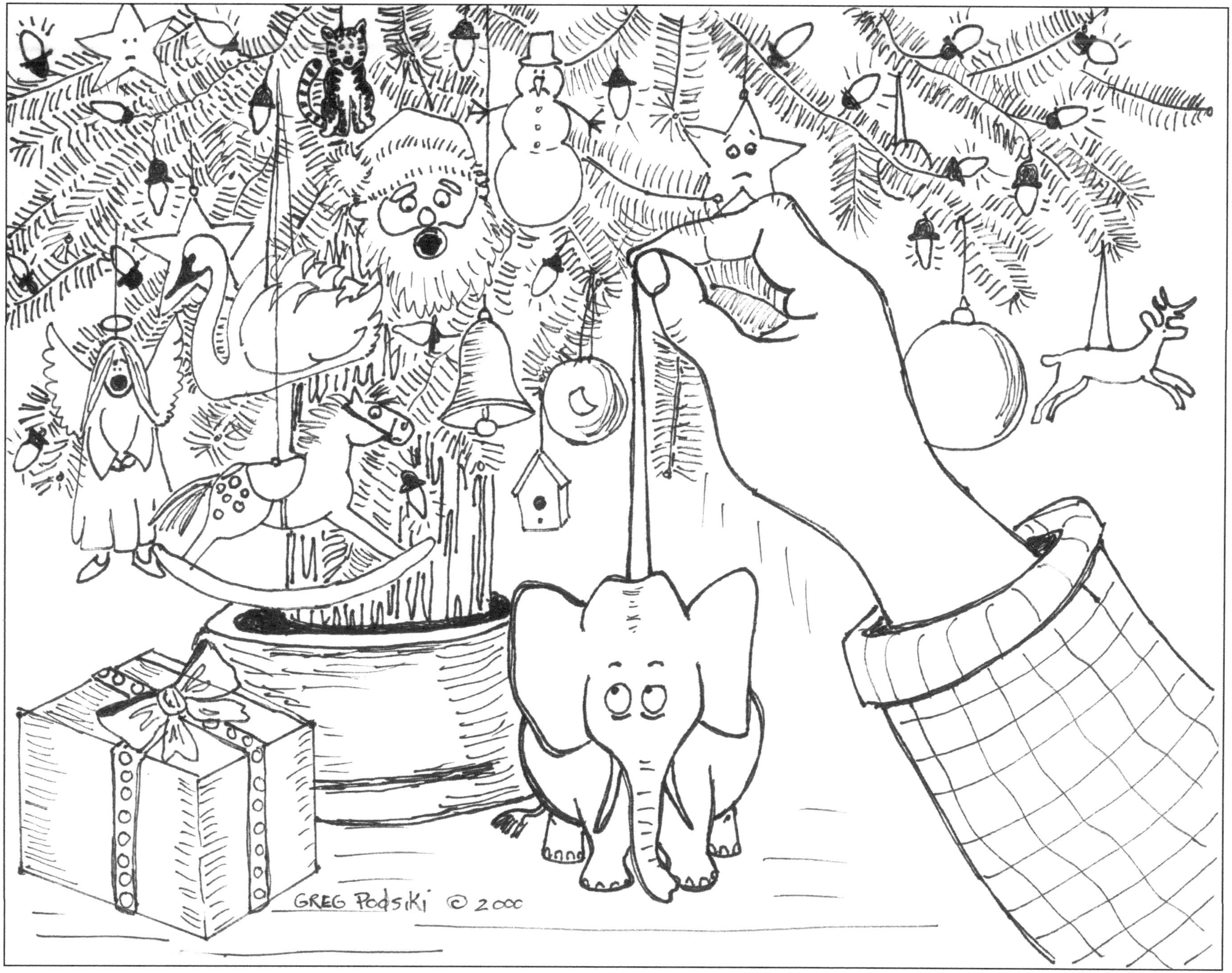
GREG PODSKI © 2000

Overload on the Christmas tree (brace yourselves – here he comes!)

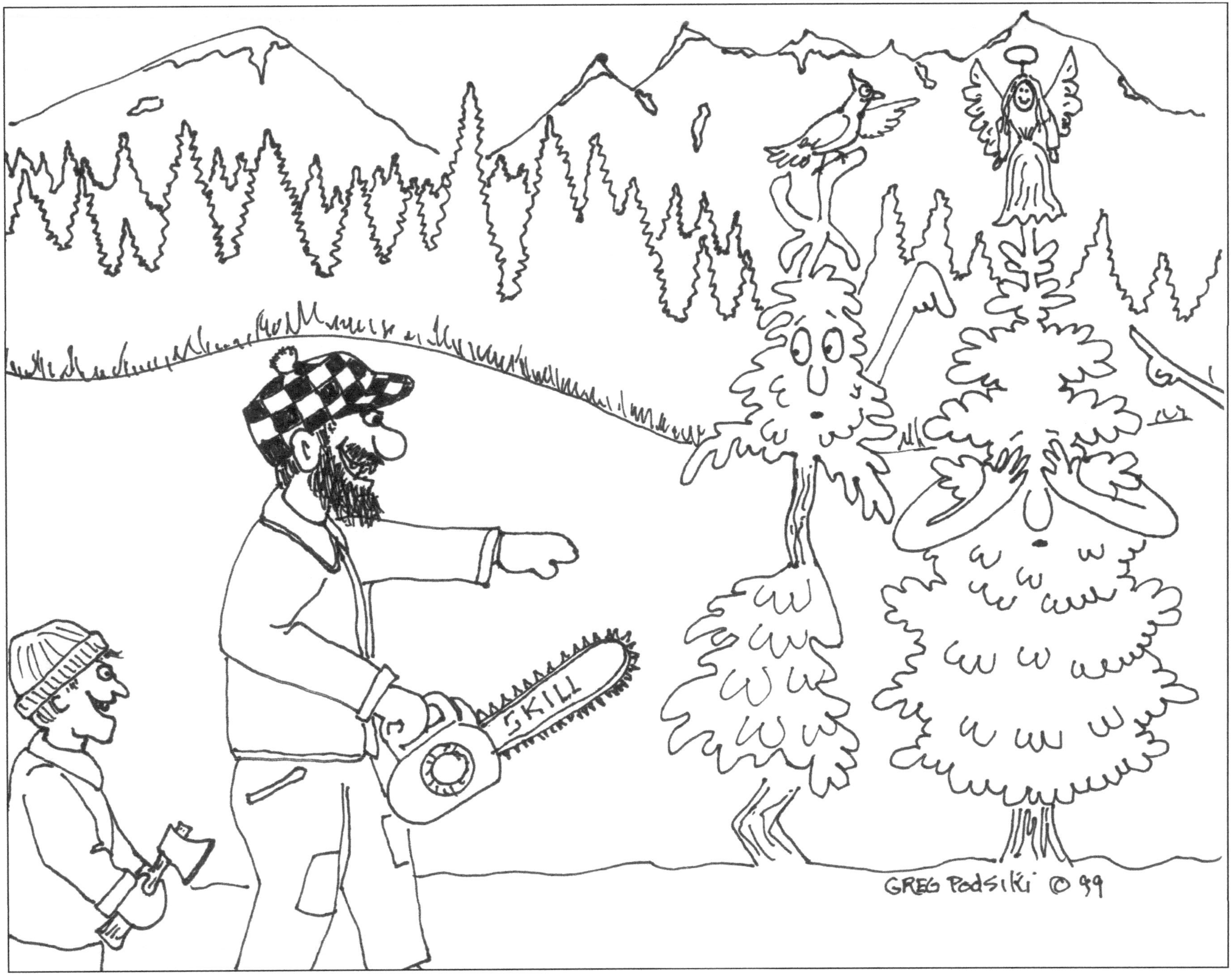
SKILL
GREG Podsiki © 99

Decisions, decisions!

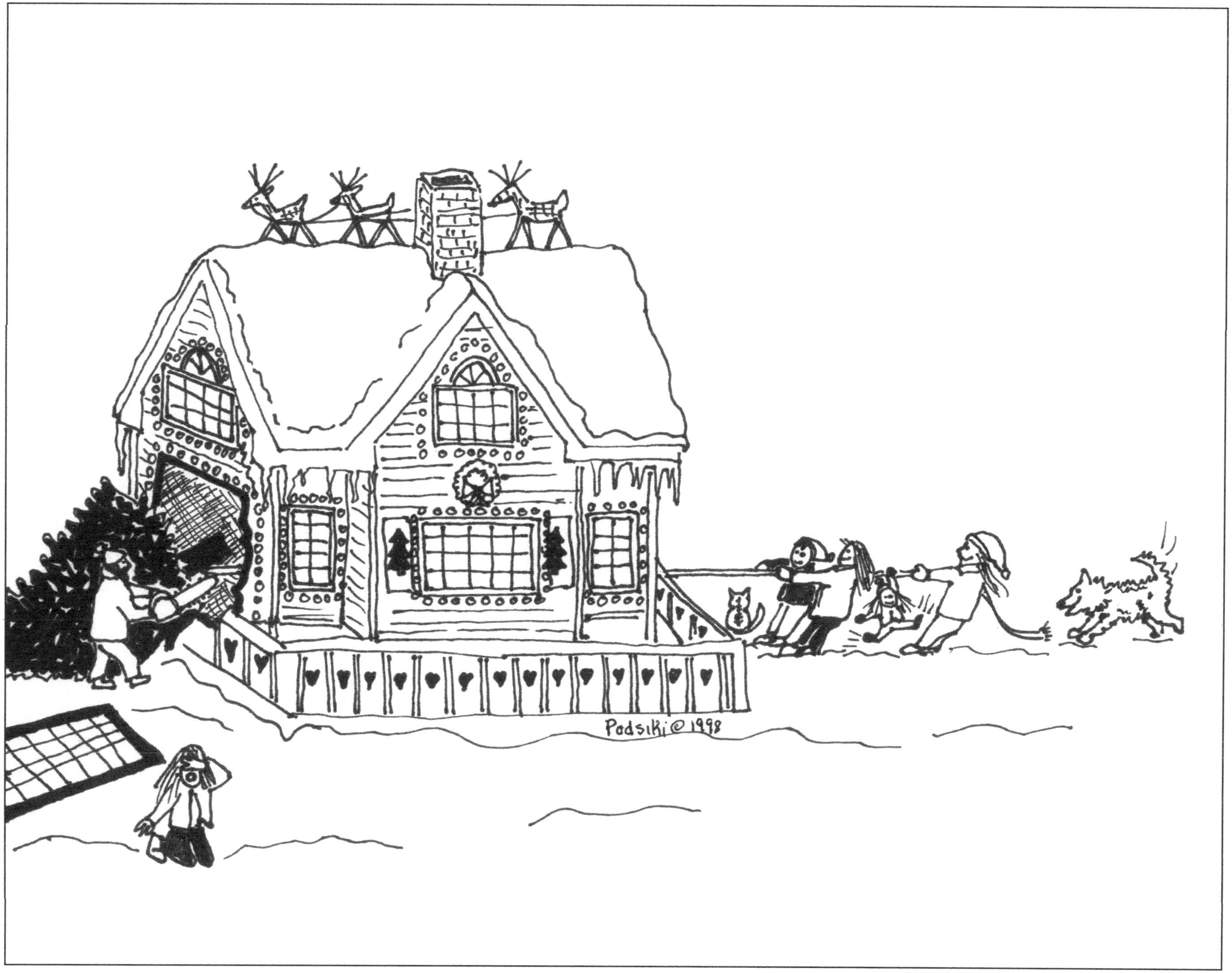
Podsiki © 1998

“Just a minute kids, I need to cut a bigger hole”

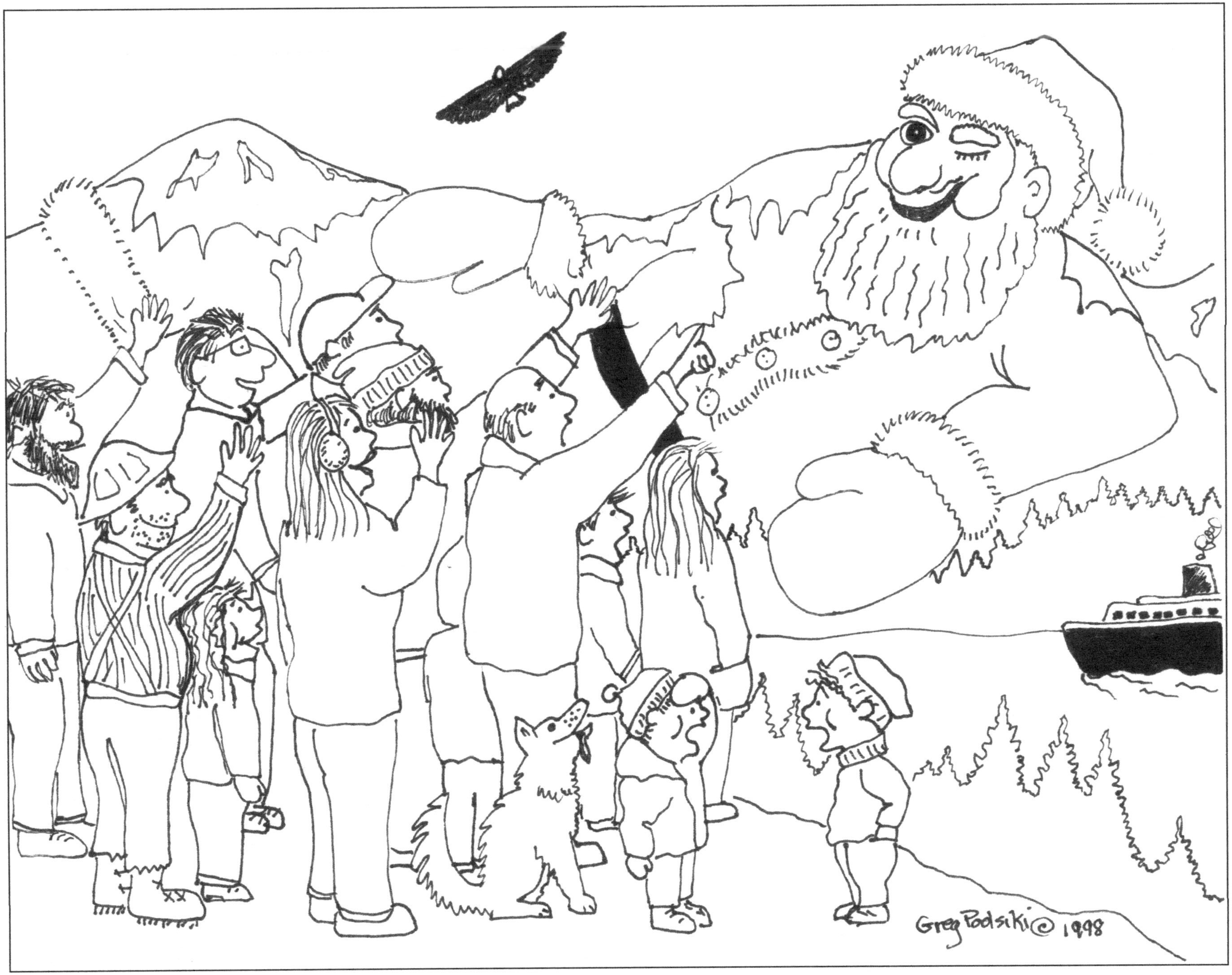
Greg Podsiki © 1998

Santa Claus (believe) mountain, Haines Alaska

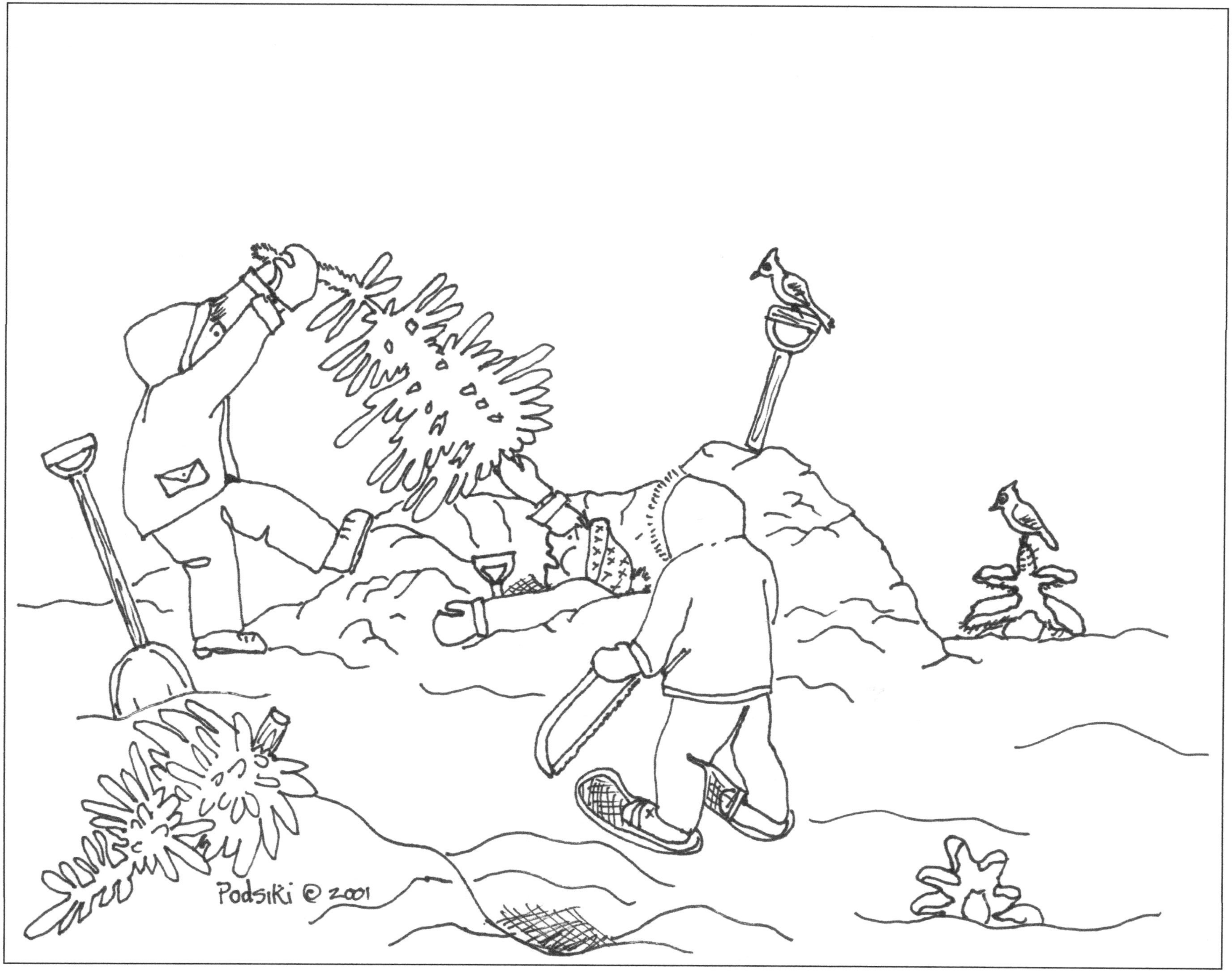
Podsiki © 2001

"Mining" for Christmas trees after the big blizzard

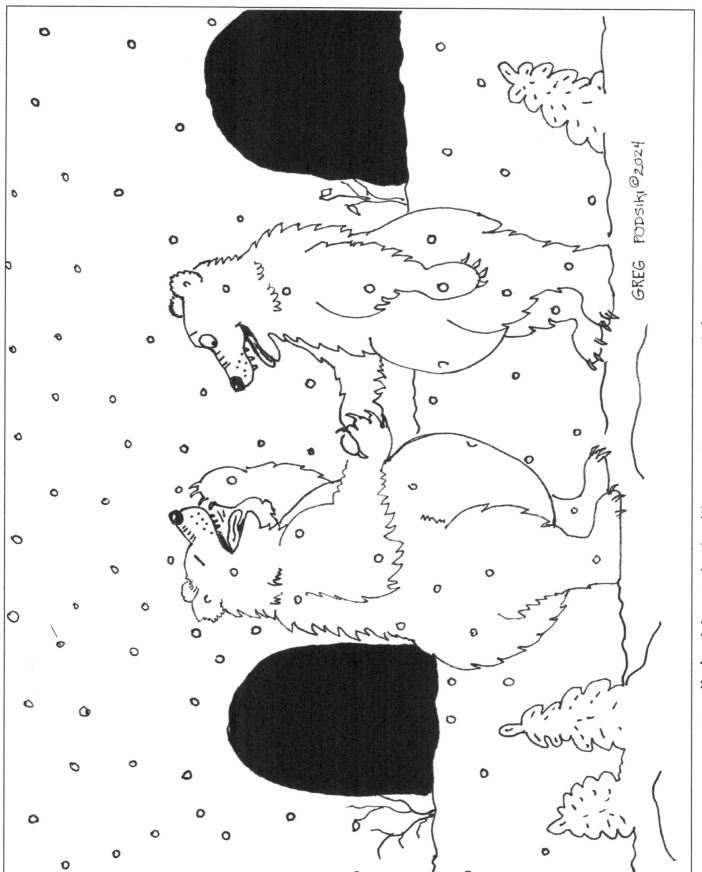

"Well, buddy, it looks like you're prepared for a long winter"

GREG PODSIKI ©2024

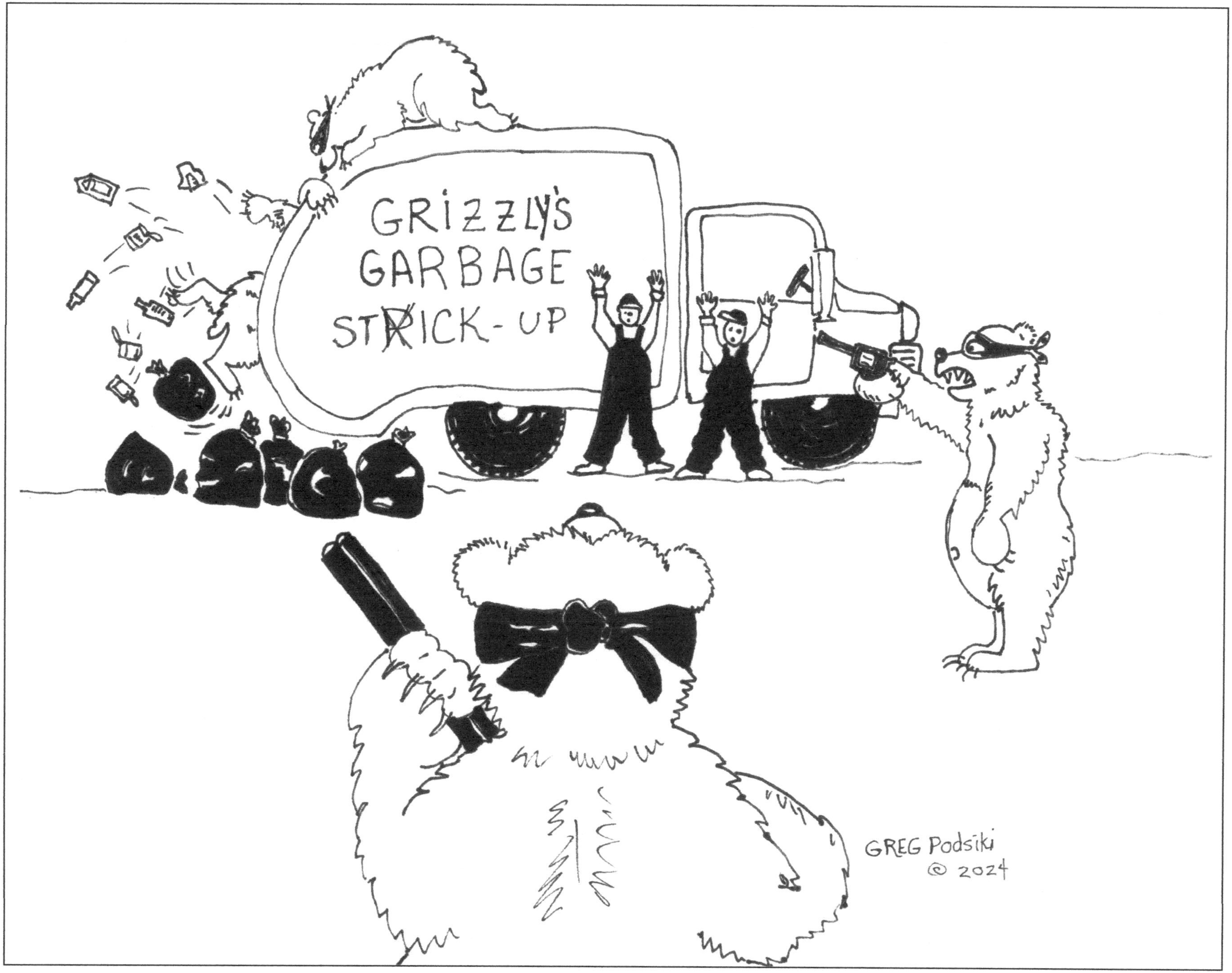
GRIZZLY'S
GARBAGE
STRICK-UP
GREG Podsiki
© 2024

Consequences of fencing the garbage dump

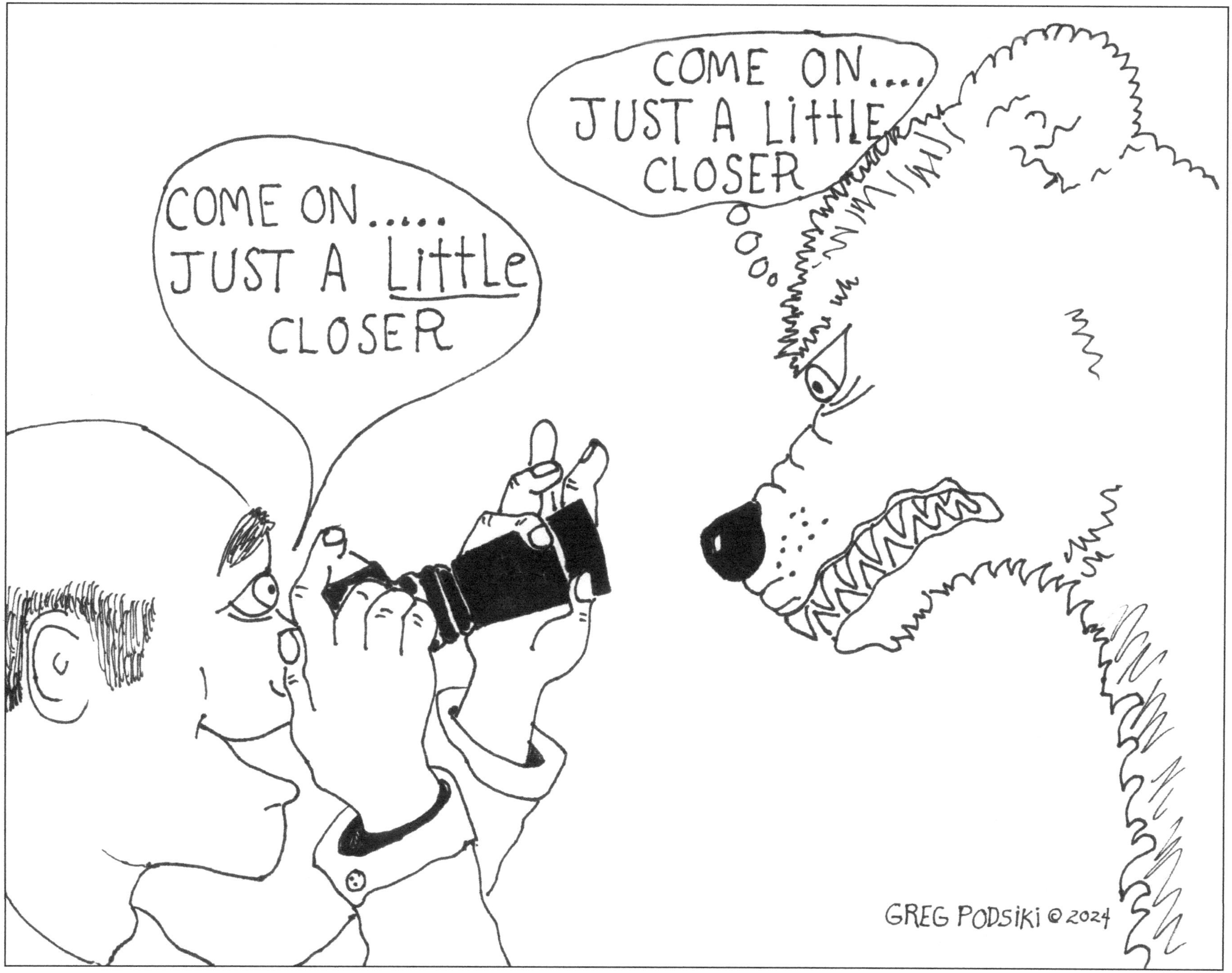
COME ON..... JUST A Little CLOSER
COME ON.... JUST A Little CLOSER
GREG PODSIKI © 2024

Another photographer gone wrong

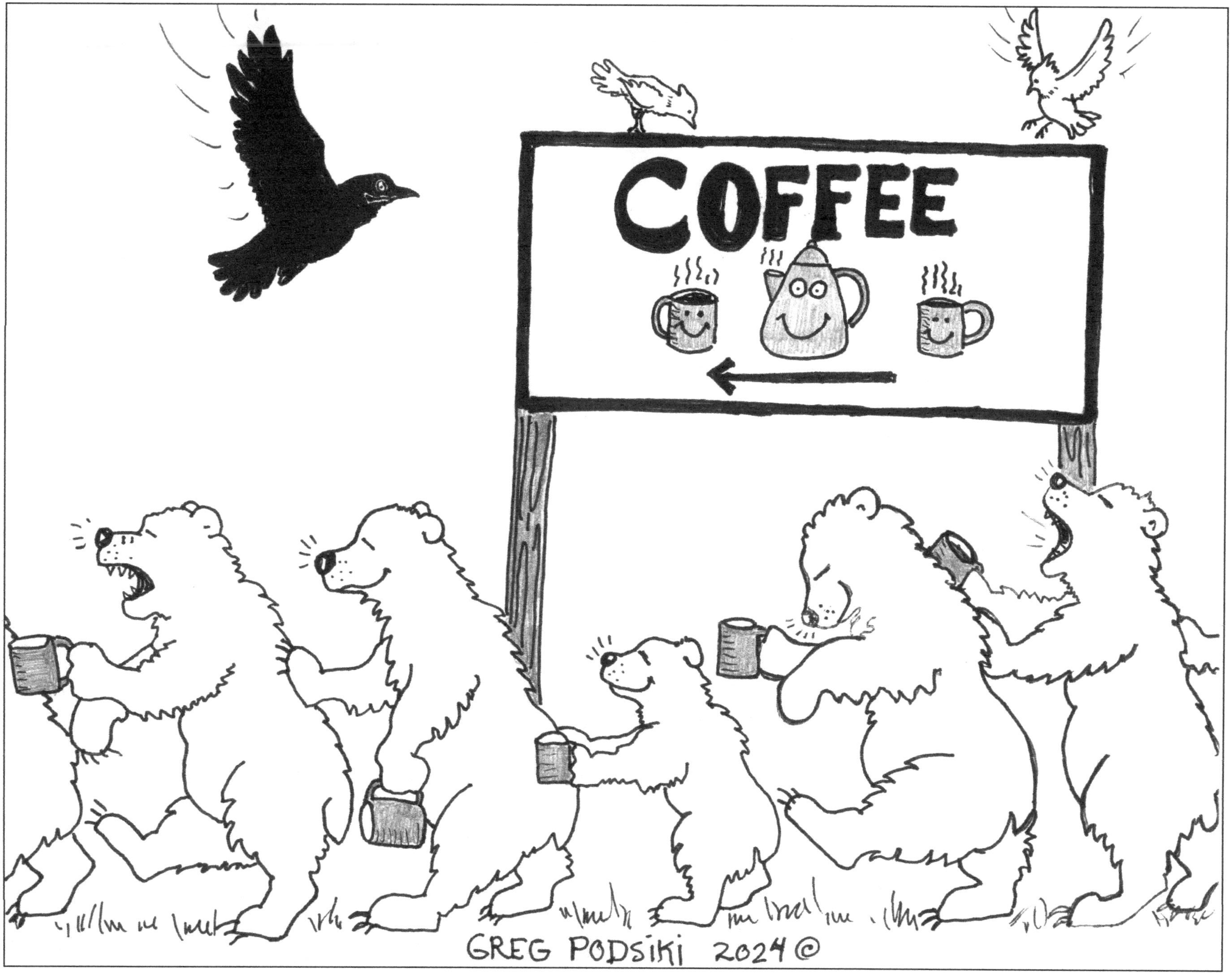
COFFEE
GREG PODSIKI 2024©

Springtime in Alaska

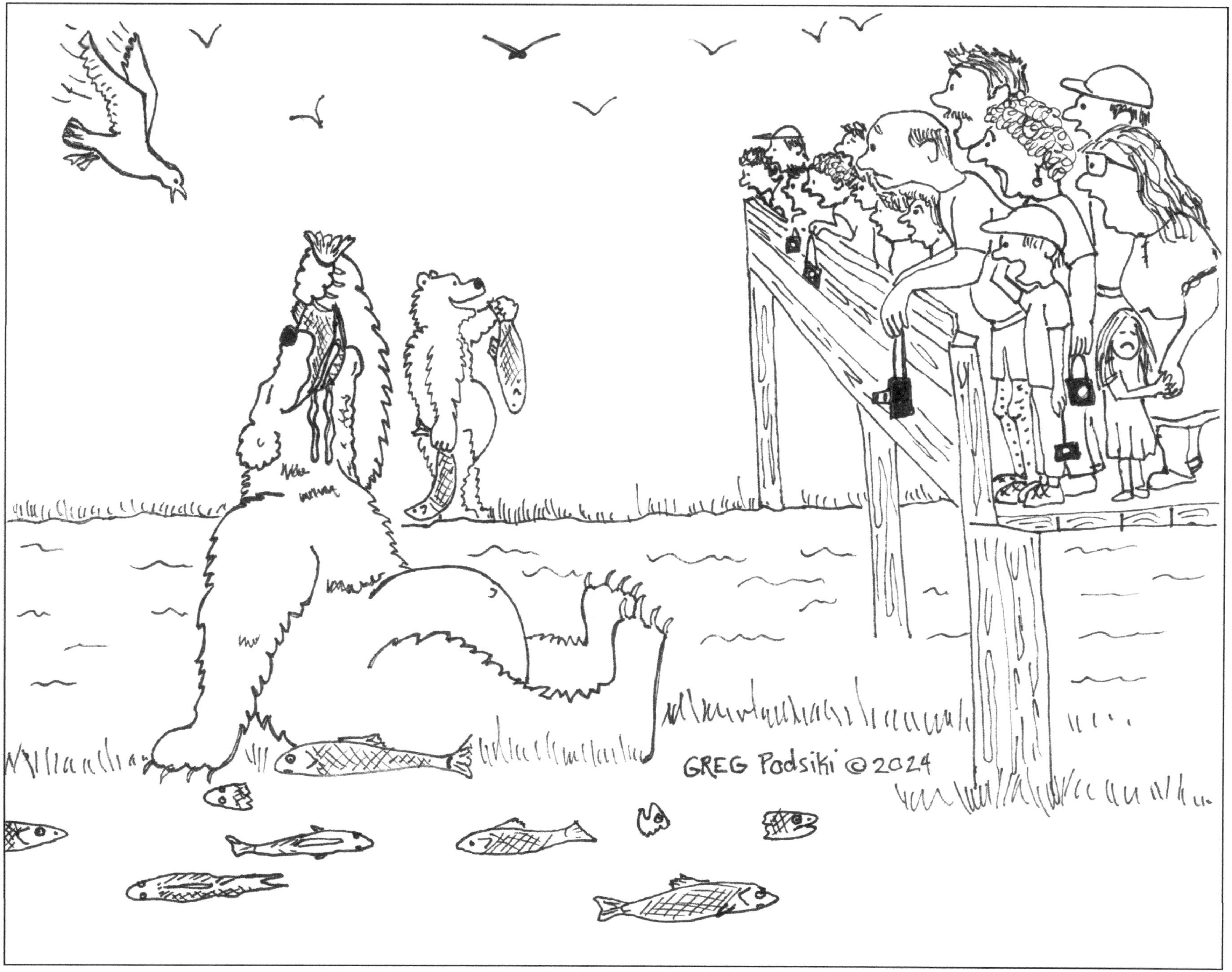
GREG Podsiki ©2024

Show offs

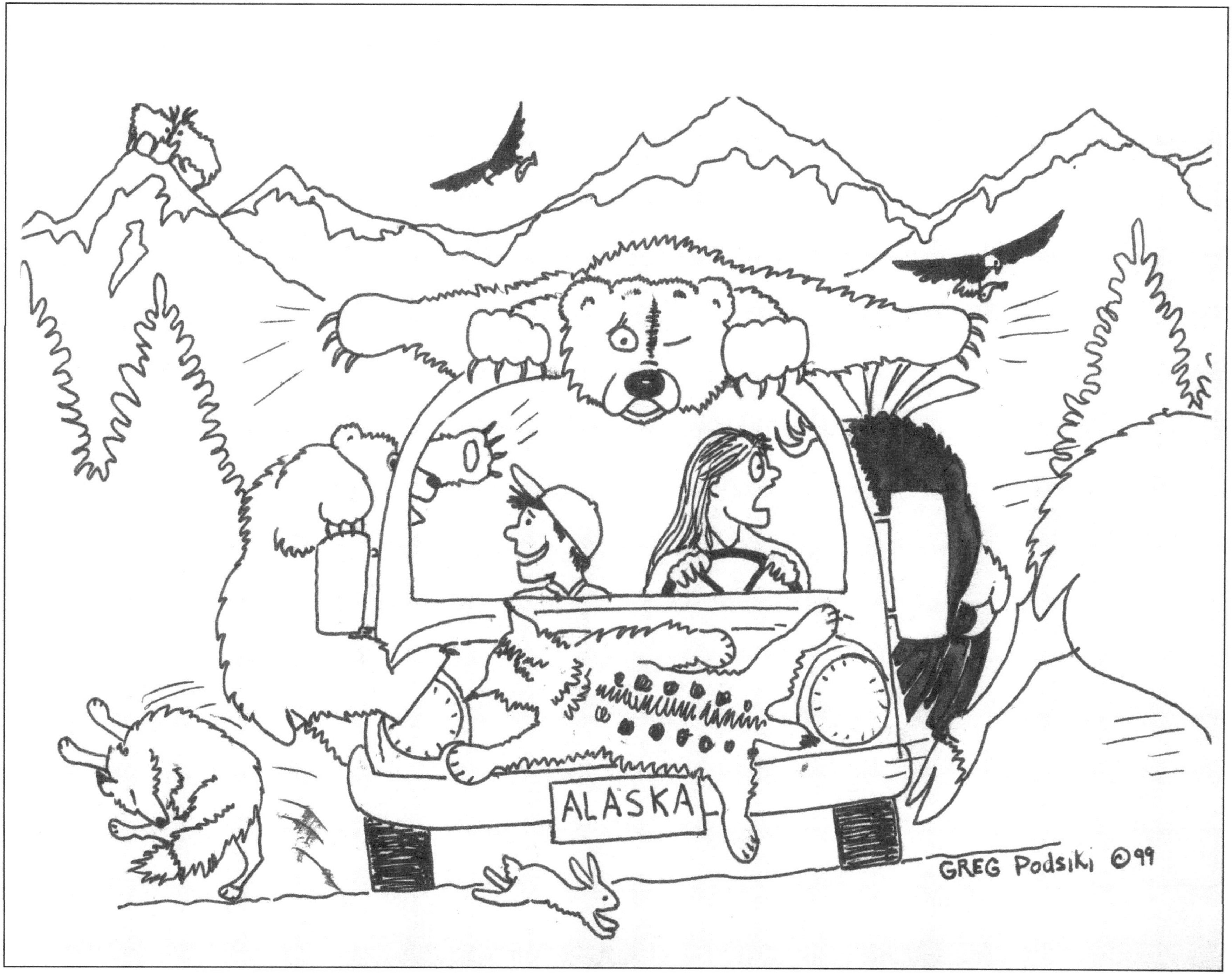
ALASKA
GREG Podsiki ©99

Taking your kid to summer camp in Alaska

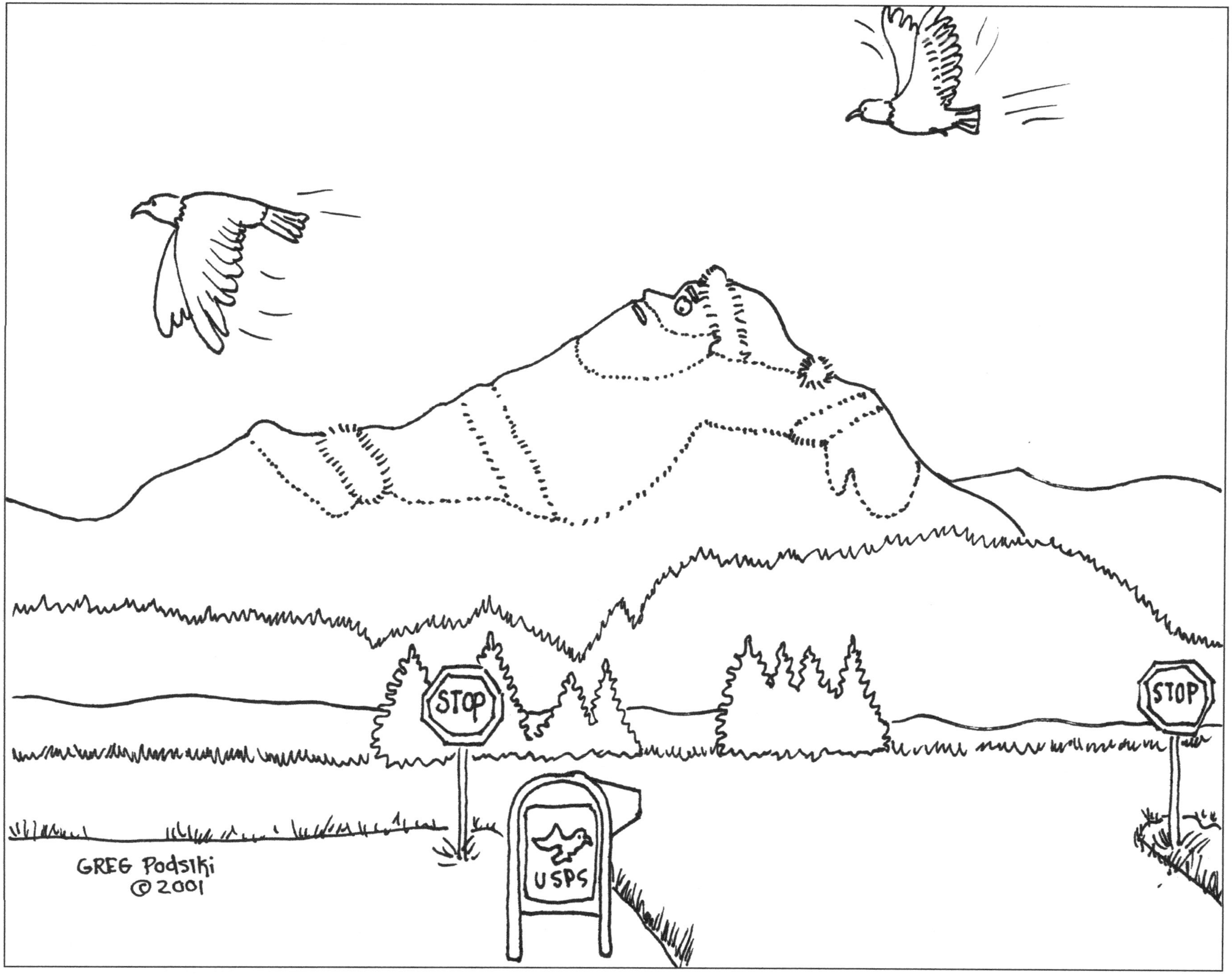
STOP
STOP
USPS
GREG Podsiki
© 2001

Imagination (Santa Claus Mountain)

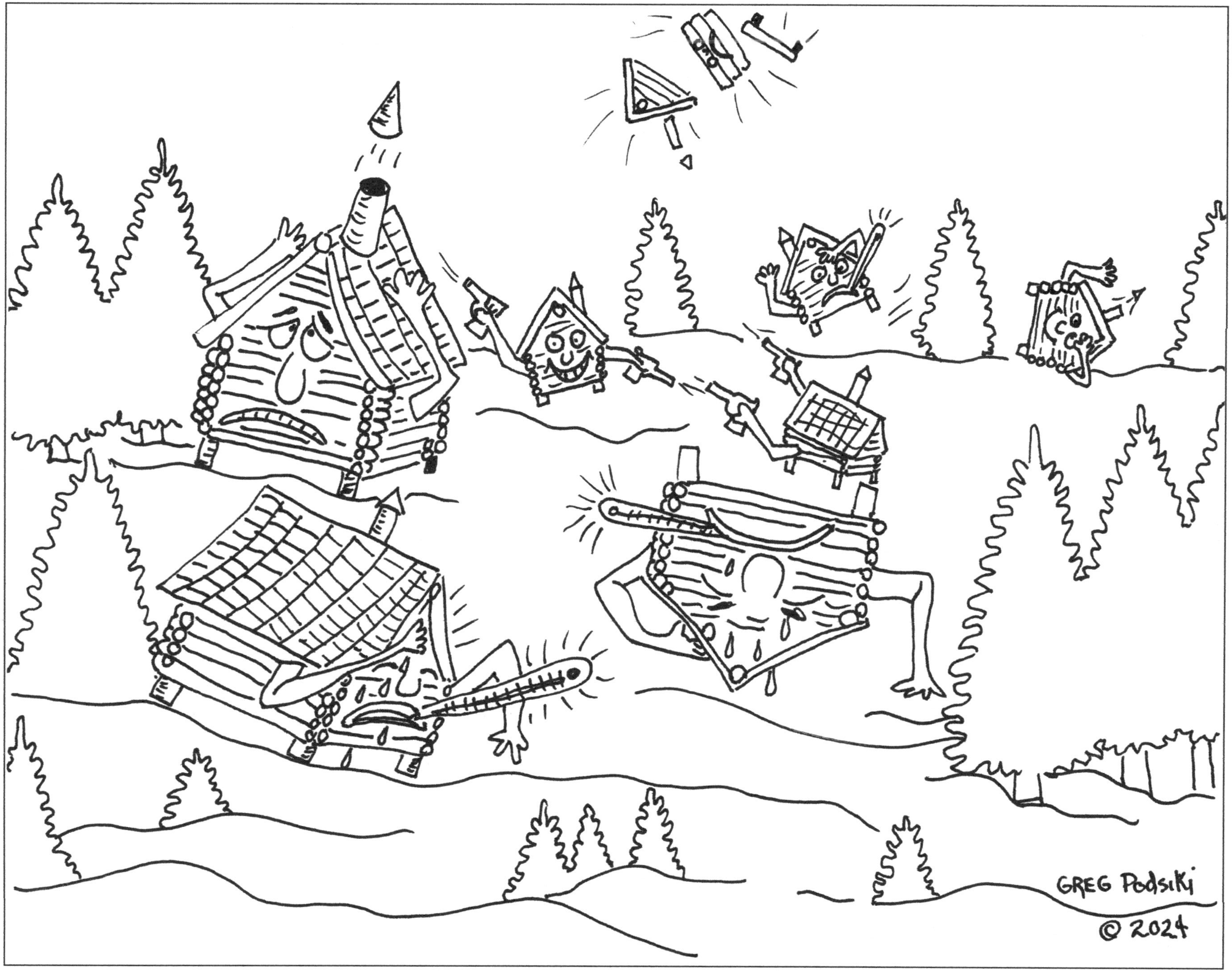
GREG Podsiki
© 2024

Cabin fever

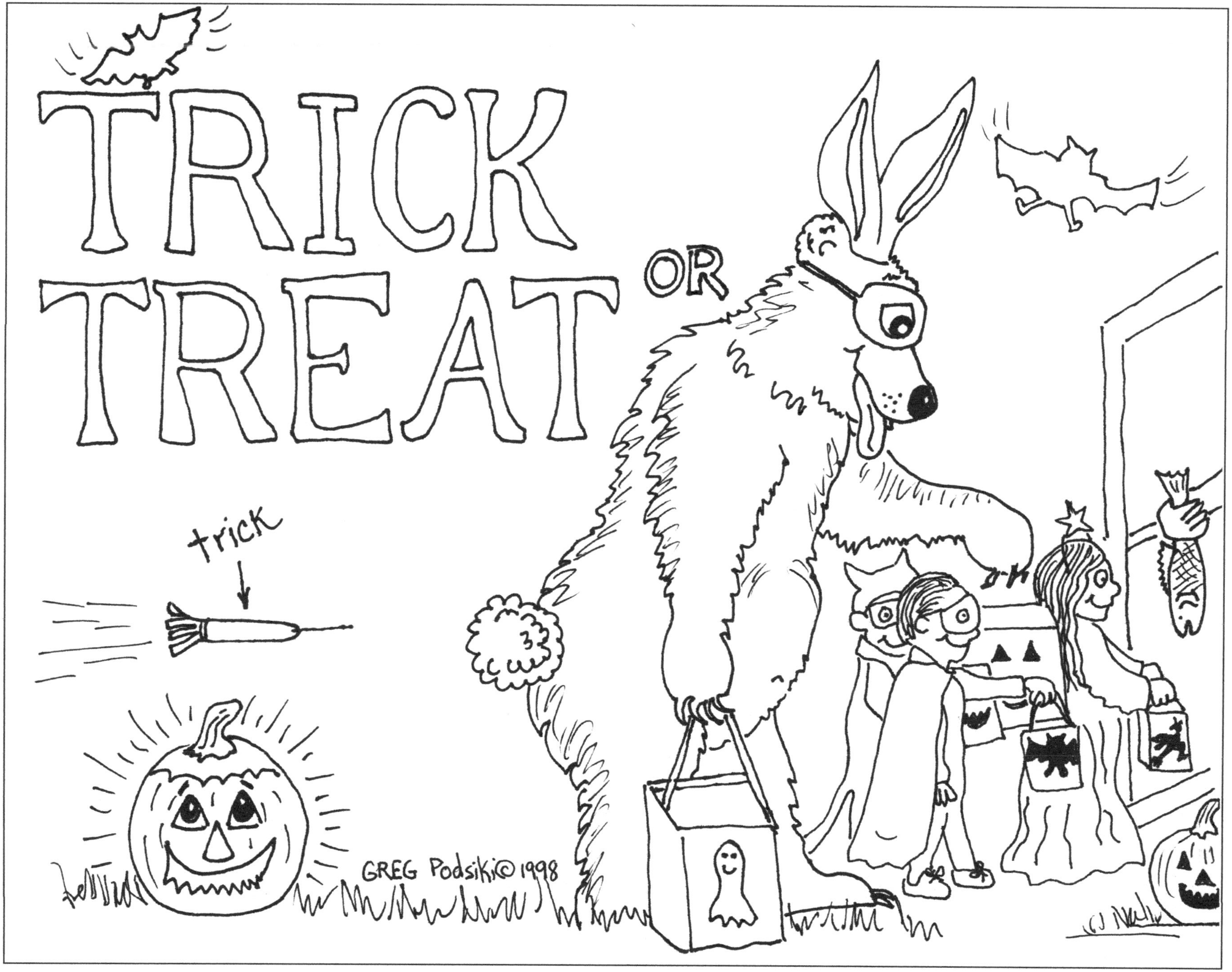
TRICK OR TREAT
trick
GREG Podsiki© 1998

Big Bunny is about to take a long nap!

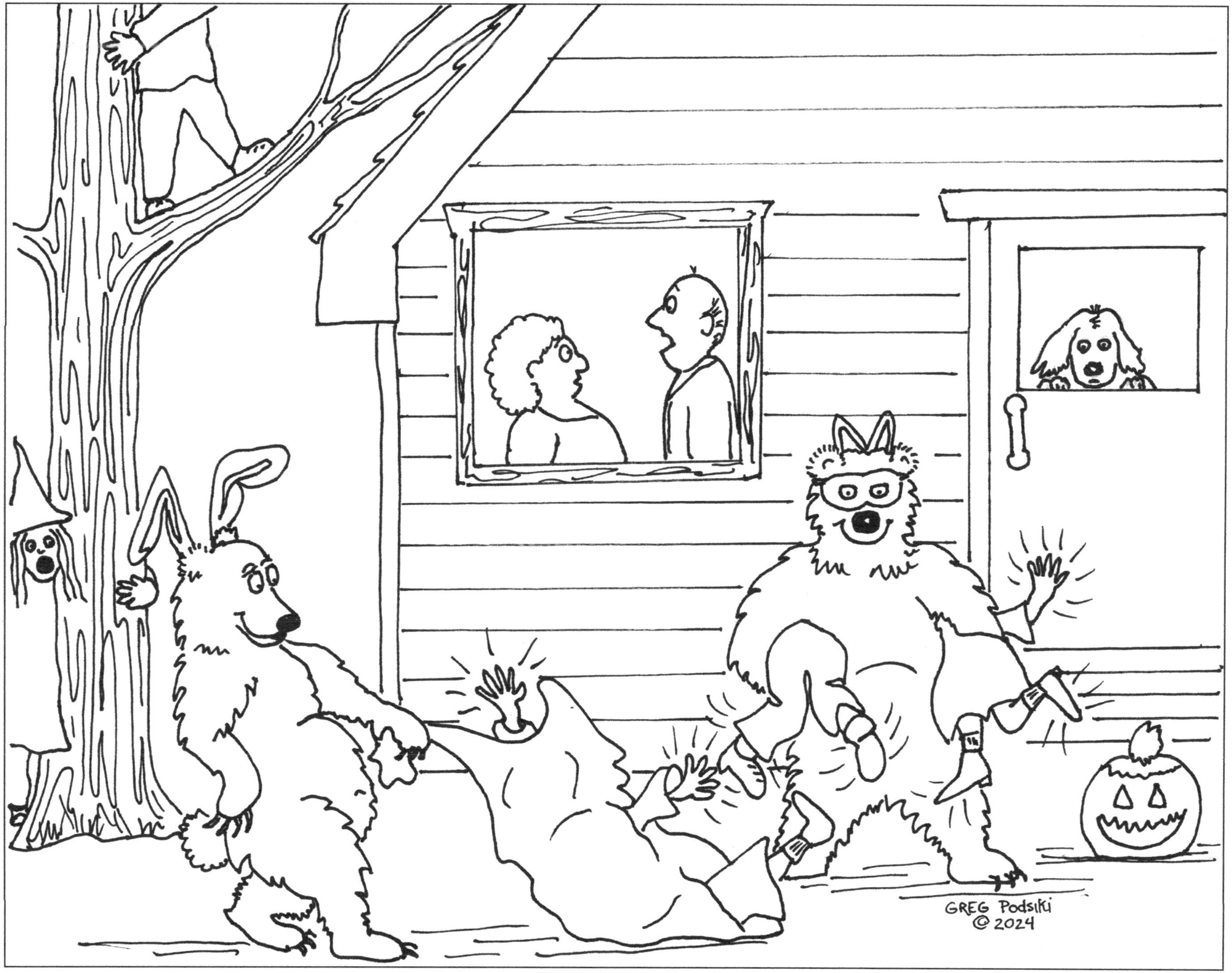
GREG Podsiki
© 2024

"What happened to all the trick-or-treaters?"

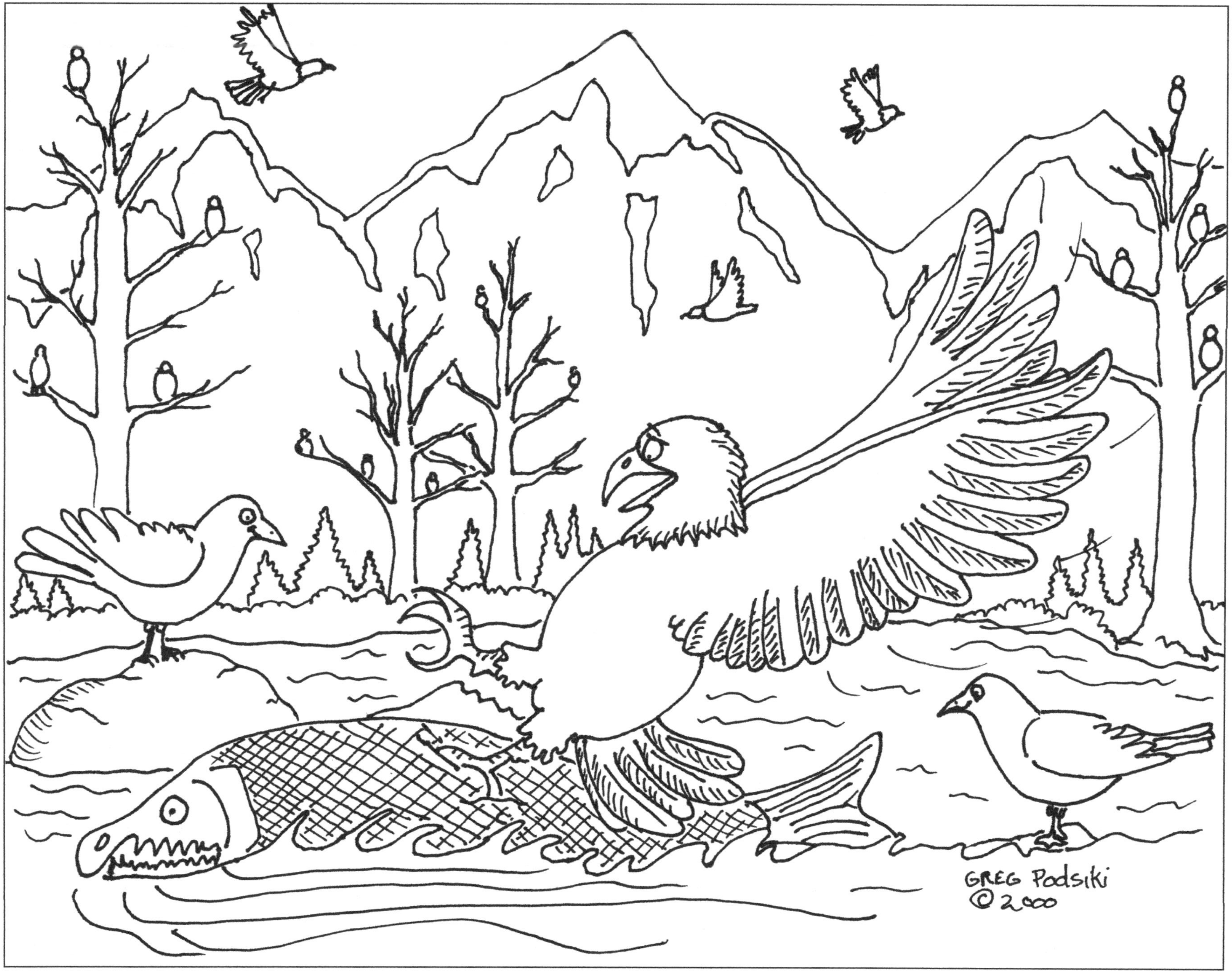
GREG Podsiki
© 2000

"HELP! I'm stuck!"

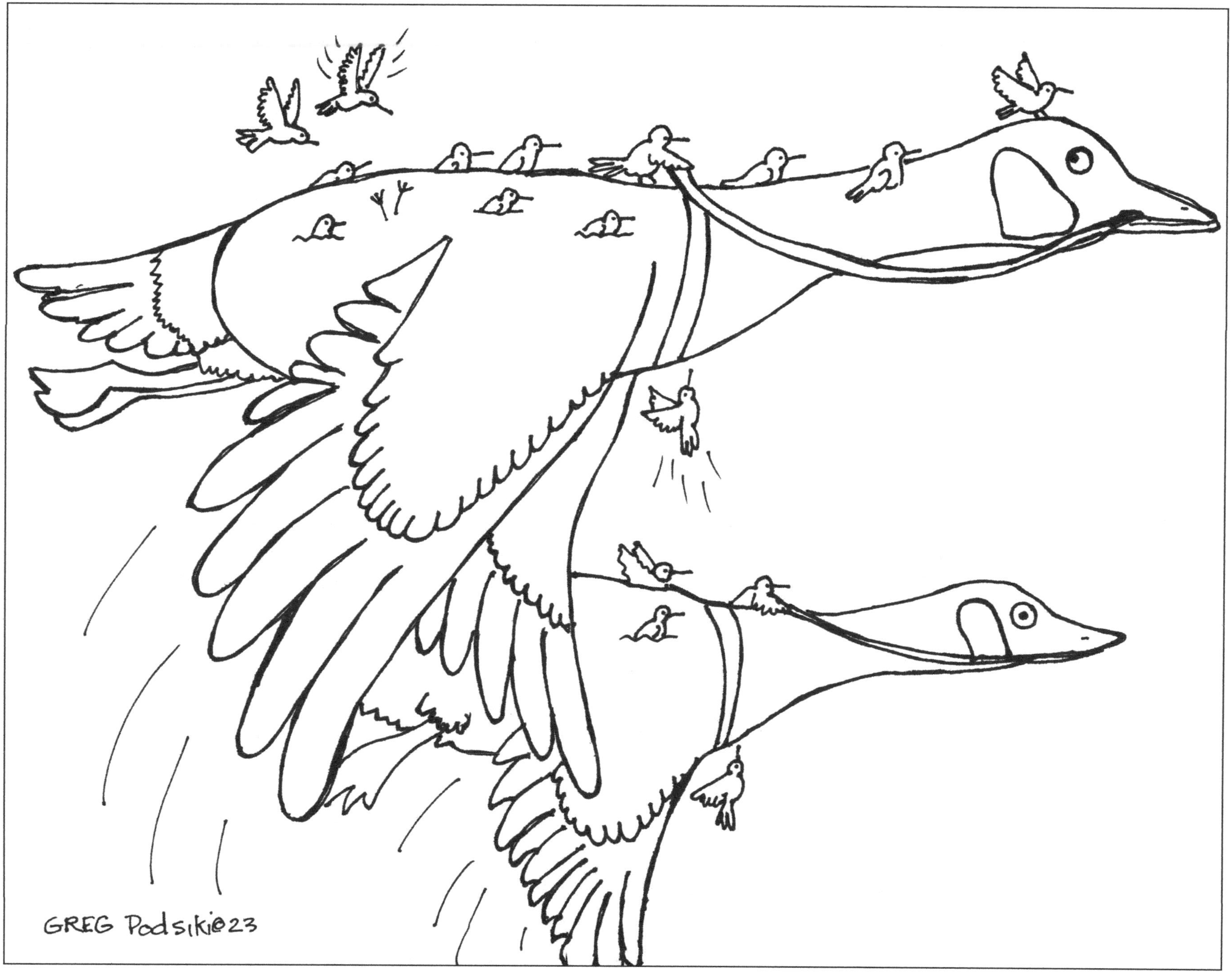
GREG Podsiki©23

How hummingbirds migrate (old wives tale)

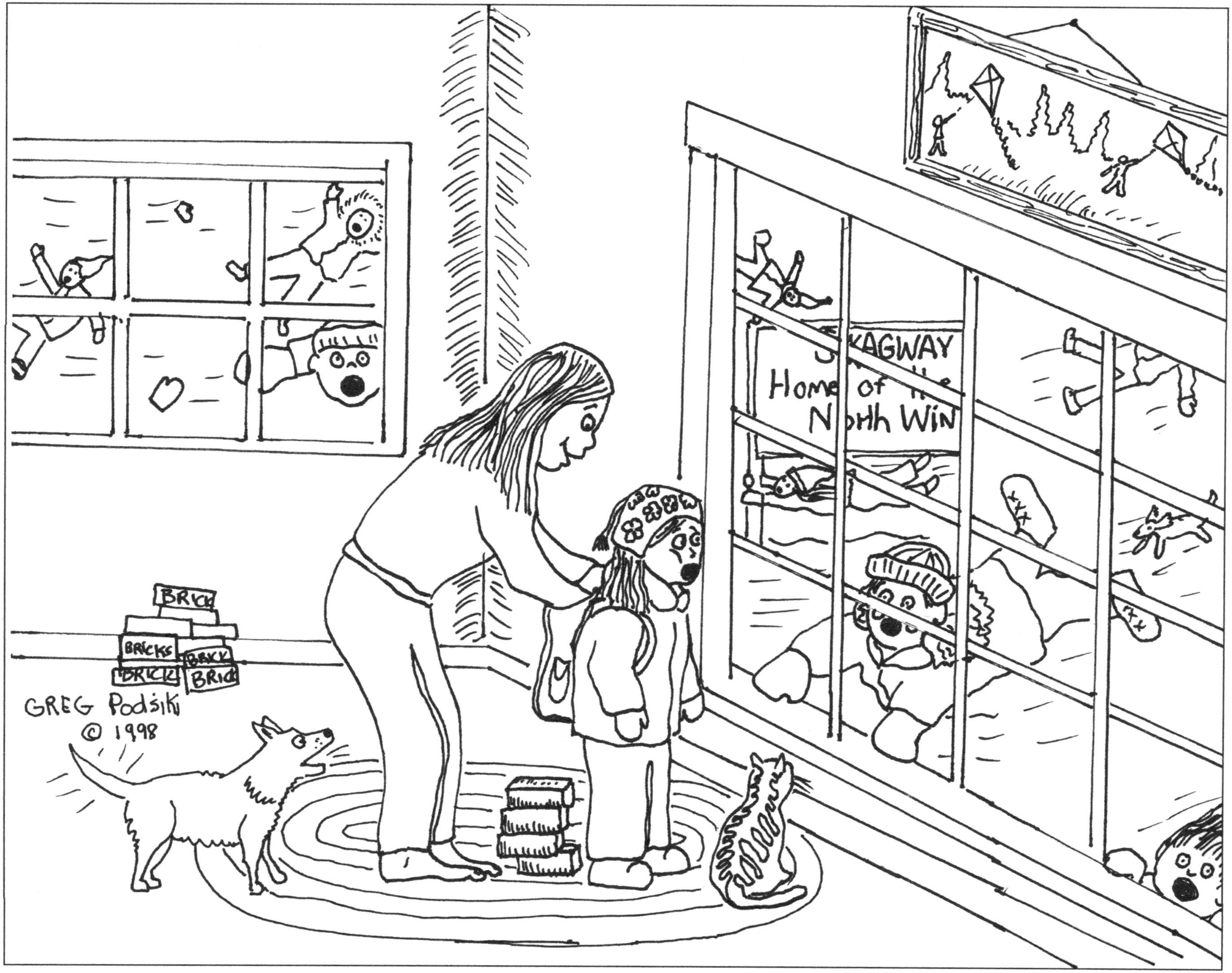
AGWAY
Home of
N rth Win
BRICK
BRICKS
BRKY
BRICK
BRICK
GREG Podsiki
© 1998

"It looks like it's a six brick day today, honey"

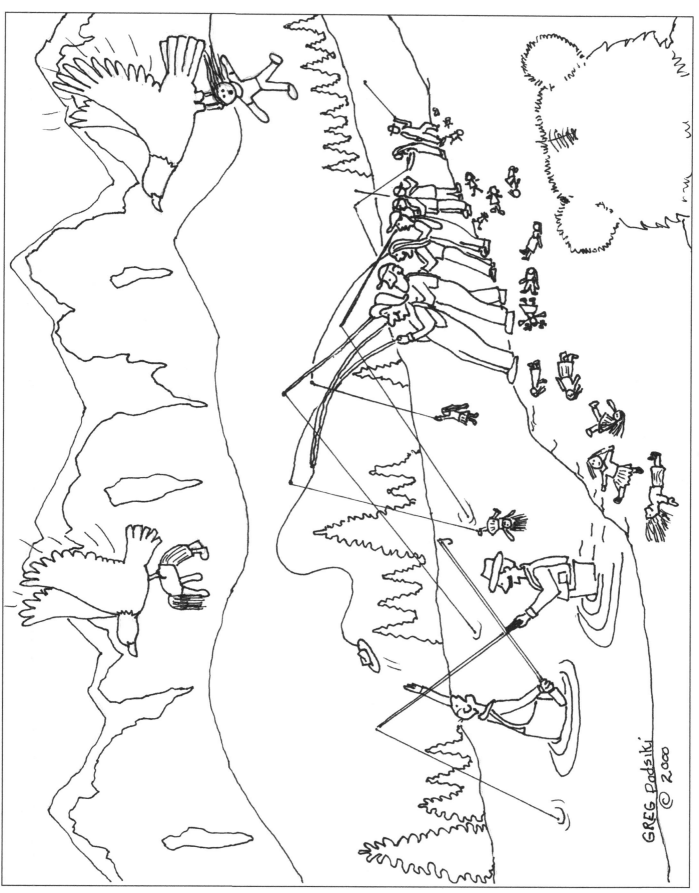

Fishing for dollies

GREG Podsiki
© 2000

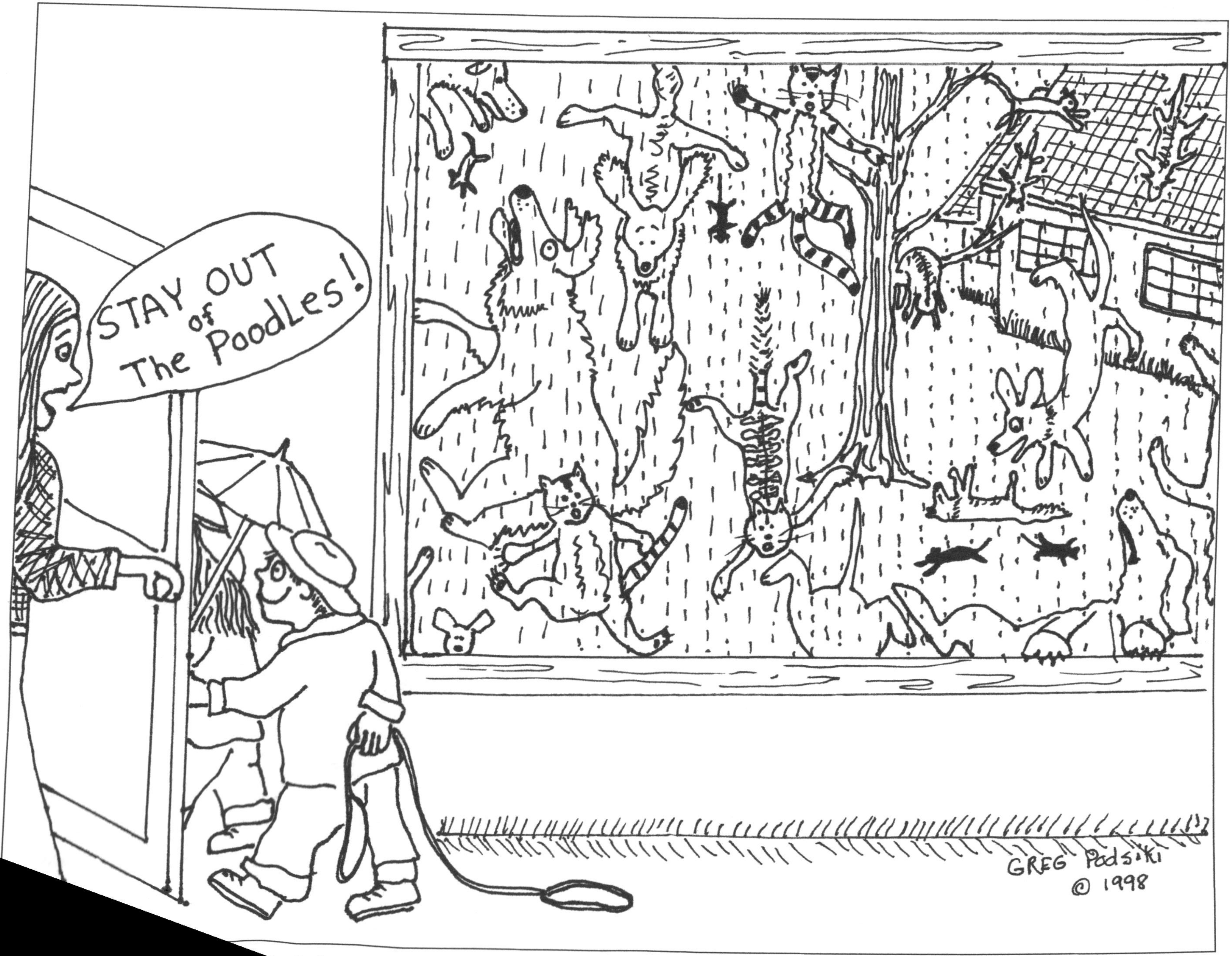
STAY OUT of The Poodles!
GREG Podsiki
© 1998

…ining cats and dogs out there! DON'T bring any home"

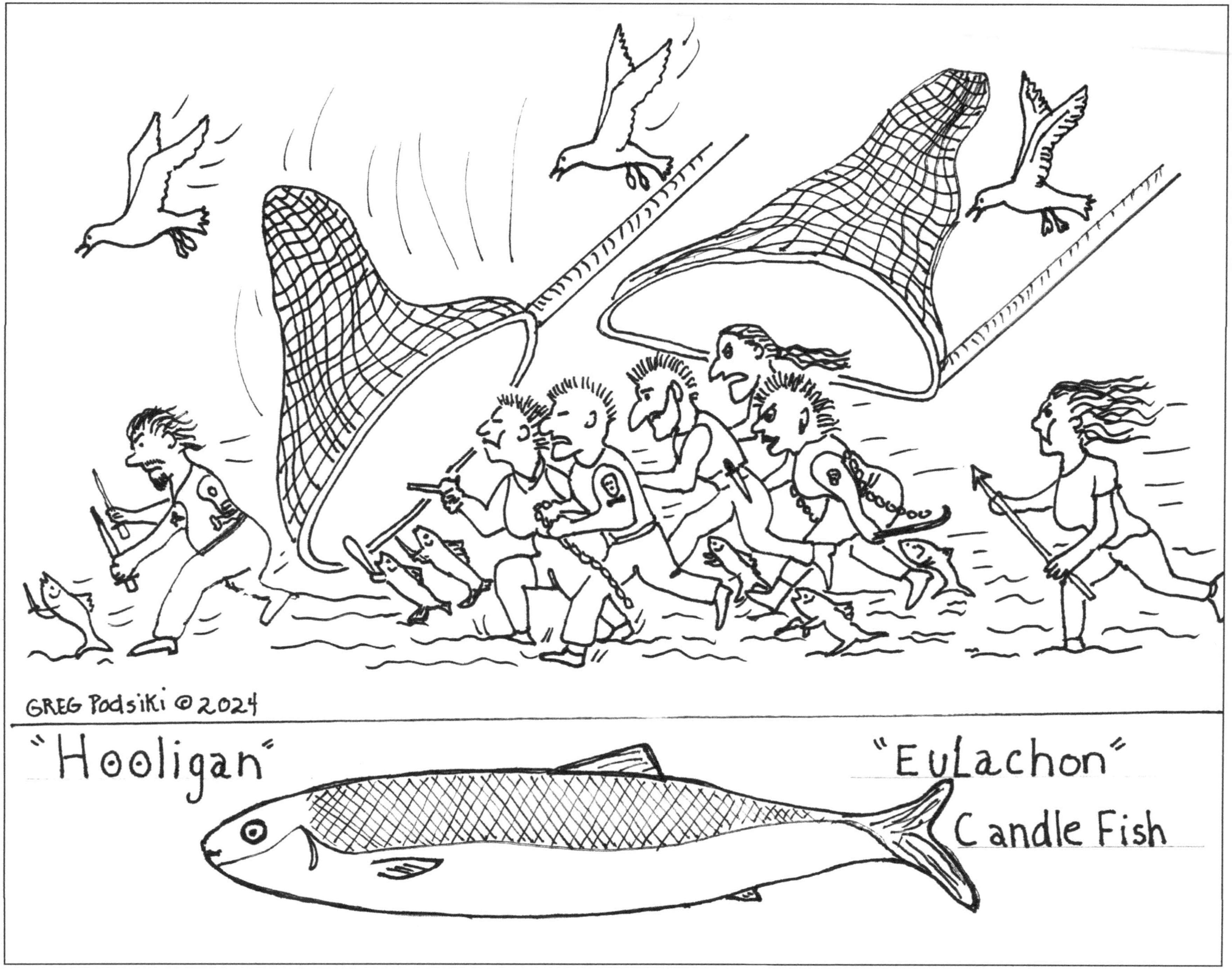
GREG Podsiki © 2024
"Hooligan"
"EuLachon"
Candle Fish

Dip netting for hooligan

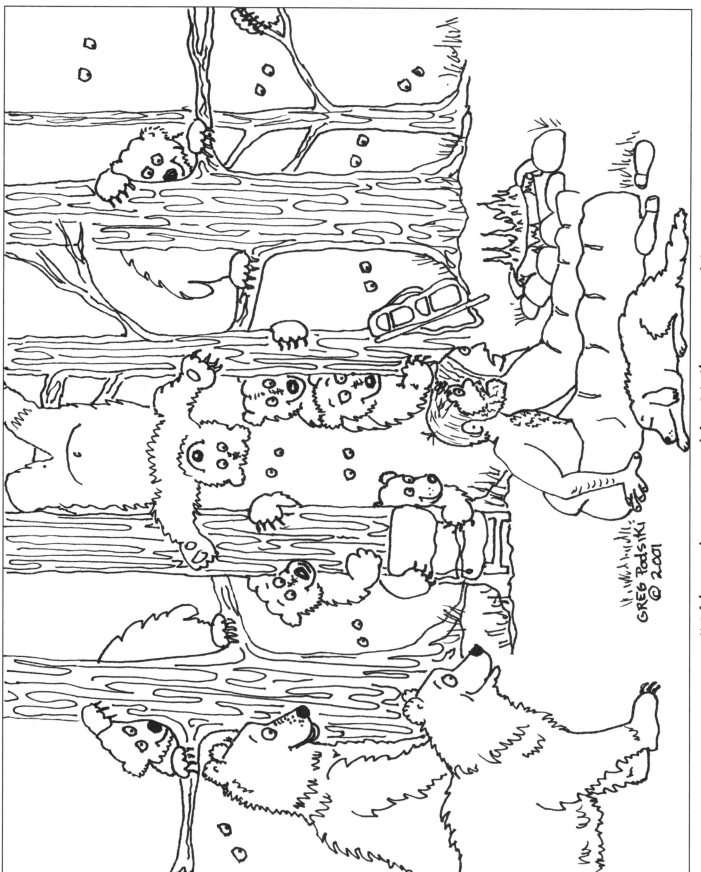

"Did you hear something?" (bear-a-noia)

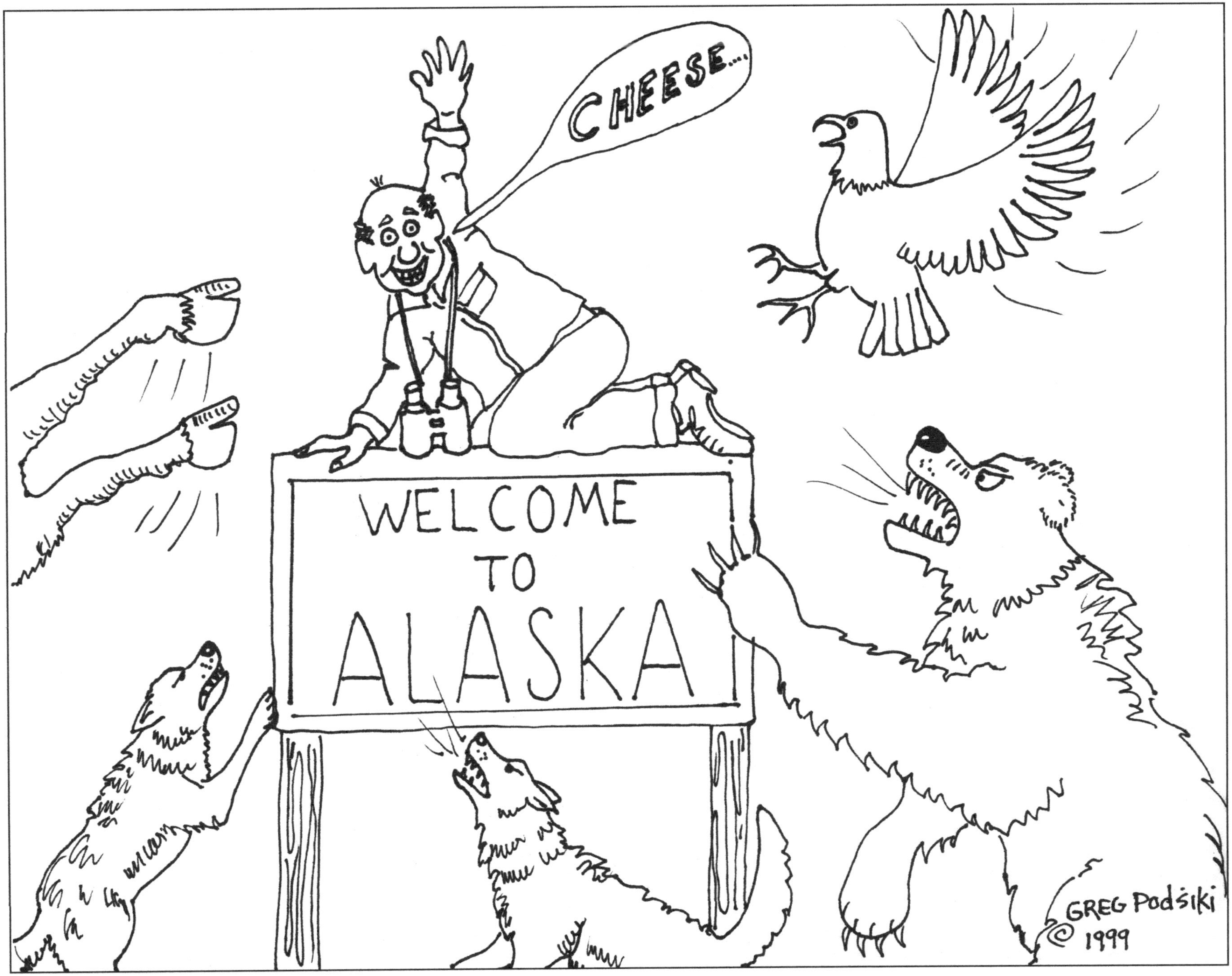
CHEESE...
WELCOME TO ALASKA
GREG Podśiki © 1999

Smile for the camera

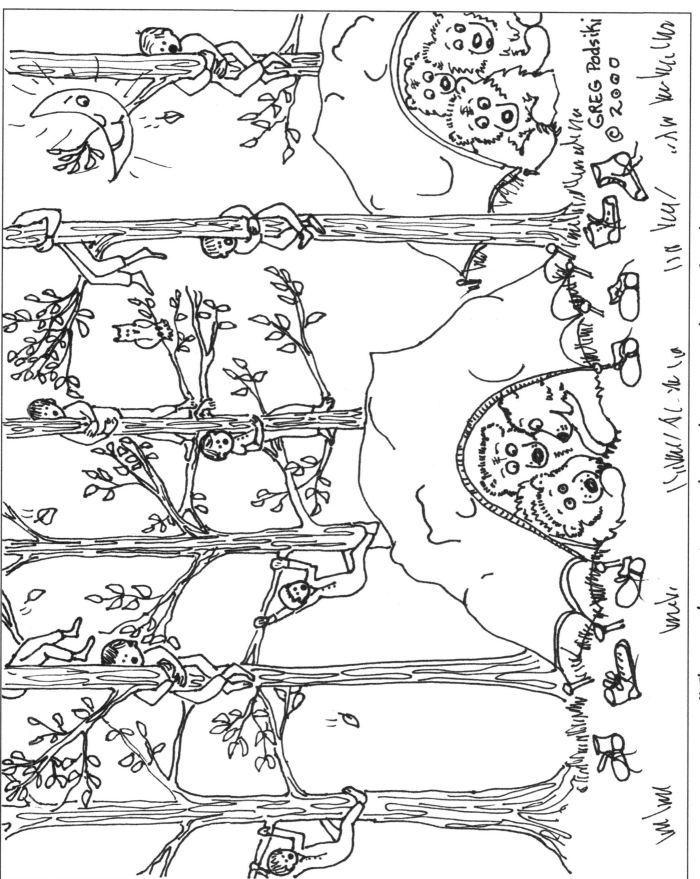

"These cub scouts sure know how to make a nice den"

GREG Podsiki © 2000

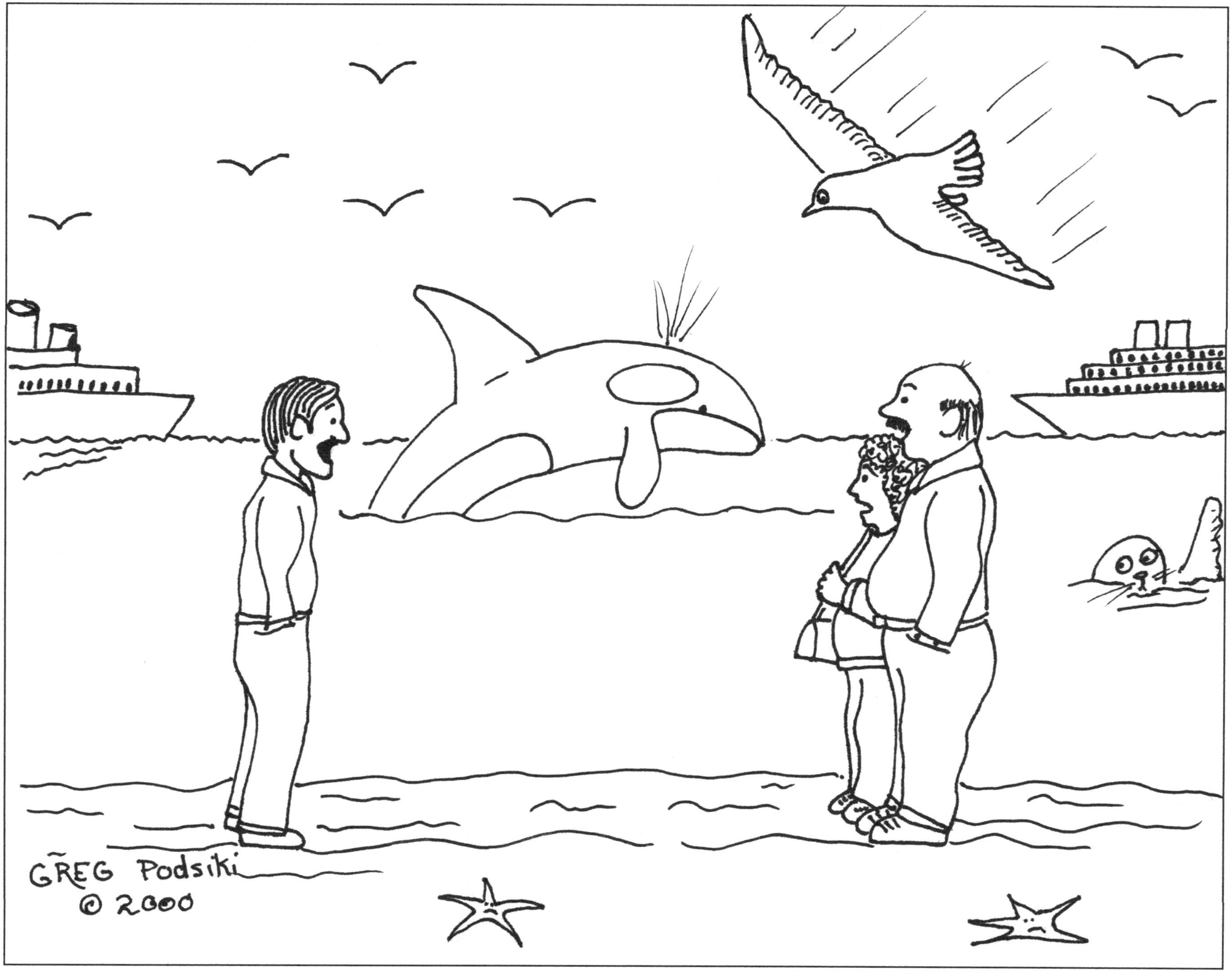
GREG Podsiki
© 2000

"Excuse me sir; do you know the elevation here?"

About the Author

Greg was raised in Rochester NY. He completed his Associates degree in Natural Resource Conservation in 1972 at Finger Lakes Community College in Canandaigua NY. At the age of 20 he transfered to the University of Alaska in Fairbanks to continue his studies in Wildlife Management. In 1979 he moved to Haines Alaska. He has combined his love for wildlife, drawing, and sense of humor in his art for his entire adult life. For years Greg has been encouraged by his many friends, neighbors, and family members to print his cartoons. After retiring from the Haines Post Office in 2022, he has finally found the time to sort through his hundreds of cartoons as well as to produce more for his first book. It was his children, and grandchildren that insisted his first book of cartoons be a coloring book for all ages. South East Alaska is a popular destination for cruise ship passengers and other visitors who are intrigued with the unique life style that rural Alaskans encounter in their daily lives, and they will enjoy this book every bit as much as Alaskan residents.

To see more of Greg's cartoons and illustrations you can visit his website, thealaskasidecartoons.com

About the Book

Over the years Greg's four children have spent many hours sitting at the kitchen table watching their dad draw cartoons for a local weekly paper as well as drawing designs for business logos, and t shirts for special small town events, that his wife would hand silk screen. He made copies for them to enjoy coloring, and now his 9 grandchildren have the same opportunity. Turning his cartoons into an actual coloring book seems like the natural way to share his art, as well as the humor of the unique Alaskan life, for both visitors and residents alike. Adults will enjoy coloring these cartoons just as much as the kids.